UNDERSTANDING CONFLICT AND WAR

VOLUME 3

CONFLICT IN PERSPECTIVE

UNDERSTANDING CONFLICT AND WAR

VOLUME 3

CONFLICT IN PERSPECTIVE

R. J. Rummel
University of Hawaii

 SAGE PUBLICATIONS   Beverly Hills/London

For information address:

SAGE PUBLICATIONS, INC.
275 South Beverly Drive
Beverly Hills, California 90212

SAGE PUBLICATIONS LTD
28 Banner Street
London EC1Y 8QE

Printed in the United States of America

Library of Congress Cataloging in Publication Data

Rummel, R J
    Understanding conflict and war.

    Includes bibliographical references and indexes.
    CONTENTS: v. 1. The dynamic psychological field.
—v. 2. The conflict helix. —v. 3. Conflict in
perspective.
    1. International relations. I. Title.
JX1291.R8   327   74-78565
ISBN 0-8039-0855-5

FIRST PRINTING

CONTENTS

To Freedom and Dignity,
With Peace.

ACKNOWLEDGEMENTS

Again, the clarity wrung from my prose by the thorough editing of my wife, Grace, must be acknowledged. For this and tolerating my odd writing schedule, my loving thanks.

Science appears but what in truth she is,
Not as glory and our absolute boast,
But as a succedaneum, and a prop
To our infirmity. . . .
            . . . .that false secondary power
By which we multiply distinctions, then
Deem that our puny boundaries are things
That we perceive, and not that we have made.

                    Wordsworth, *The Prelude* II

Chapter 1

INTRODUCTION AND SUMMARY

Peace makes plentie, plentie makes pride,
Pride breeds quarrell, and quarrell brings warre:
Warre brings spoile, and spoile povertie,
Povertie pacience, and pacience peace:
So peace brings warre and warre brings peace.

George Puttenham,
The Art of English Poesie, 1589

1.1 INTRODUCTION

This is the third volume in my attempt to understand *fundamentally* conflict, violence, and war. The first volume, *The Dynamic Psychological Field,* is concerned wholly with the psychological roots of conflict and the philosophical framework. As such, it is a self-contained, psychophilosophical analysis of man, focusing on the nature of a field perspective; perception; expectations and behavior; motivations; intentionality; the self, will, and freedom; and, finally, intentional humanism as the ethical basis for this understanding.

Field is the fundamental orienting concept for me. It is dynamic and holistic, involving a continuous spread through psychological space of energy or potentiality that is the seat of psychological forces. Man is seen individually as this dynamic psychological field of dispositions and powers, and mankind collectively appears as a dialectical balance of these individual fields.

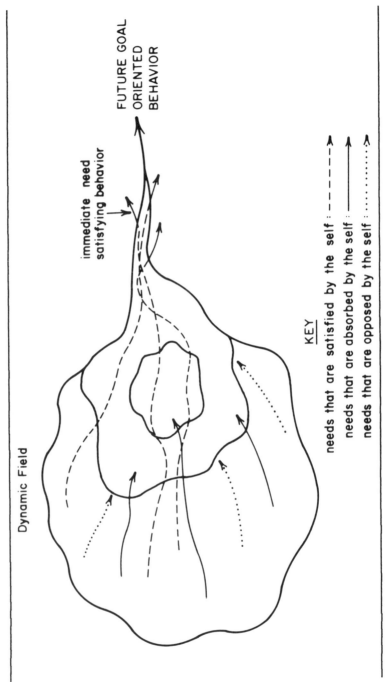

Dynamic Field

immediate need
satisfying behavior

FUTURE GOAL
ORIENTED
BEHAVIOR

KEY

needs that are satisfied by the self : – – – – –➤

needs that are absorbed by the self : ────➤

needs that are opposed by the self : ⋯⋯⋯➤

Figure 1.1

Through this field orientation, perception is an active balancing between man reaching out to transform reality within his perspective and the powers of reality to manifest themselves. Man is no passive victim of external powers; rather than being a dart board for stimuli, he is their active combatant. For man, conflict begins in the very act of perception.

Perception eventuates in behavior depending on three other aspects of the psychological field. One is the perceived *situation* calling for some kind of behavior. The second is man's *behavior dispositions,* or his tendency to behave in a particular way in this perceived *situation.* The third is his *expectations,* his predictions of the outcomes of his behavioral possibilities. And the fourth is his *personality.* Man's manifest—his specific—behavior is a result of the weighting of his behavioral dispositions by his expectations, and of the weighting of his personality by the situation he perceives. This is the *behavioral equation:* man behaves in a situation as he perceives it on the basis of the aspects of his personality engaged by the situation, his relevant behavioral disposition, and his expectations.

Man is not just a structure; he is an active participant in reality, a directed field. He has orienting needs, drives, goals, and interests: the seat of the dynamic potentiality of his field. Interests are energized attitudes rooted in man's major needs involving sex, hunger, gregariousness, protectiveness, curiosity, security, and self-assertion. The attitudes cluster into sentiments, of which the most important are the superego—providing each man's basic normative steerage—and self-sentiment. The self-sentiment defines attitudes clustering around man's superordinate goal, which is the enhancement, development, and maintenance of self-esteem.

Man is future-oriented. He organizes and integrates his psychological field toward enhancing his self-esteem, as illustrated in Figure 1.1. To comprehend his behavior is to identify the future goals in which man invests his esteem.

Is man then free to select his goals, determine his future, correct his deficiencies? To answer; we need an understanding of the self and will. The self is a power we come to know through confrontation with external powers and the inner forces we try to control. It is a power consisting of an ego, which coordinates and controls man's activities; a self-sentiment that through its superordinate self-esteem goal provides the perspective within which the self actualizes man's potentials; a superego consisting of the rules guiding the self.

The will is a facet of the self, exercising choice between alternatives, applying practical reason, and bringing the self to act.

Is the will then free to choose? Defining freedom as the power to generate or create actions independently, as spontaneous originality, we cannot know whether the will is free. We can, however, argue for the possibility that the same actions can be determined at the level of phenomena, thus are free at the underlying level of things-in-themselves. It is possible for reason to be independent of natural laws and causality, and to originate actions. Therefore, as a moral choice of reason, let us hypothesize man's freedom.

It is not sufficient to posit man's freedom or to describe him as a field, however. There must be an ethics integrating basic assumptions, framing solutions to man's problems. Intentional humanism is such an ethic. Its descriptive basis is man as field, and reality as potentiality actualized through man's perception; its normative basis is man as the pivotal value. At the center of reality is man's mentality, distinguished by intellectual faculties and moral capacity. This reality is given scale and perspective only by man's meanings, values, and intentions.

This brief introduction summarizes *The Dynamic Psychological Field* (Rummel, 1975). But a psychophilosophical analysis provides only part of the foundation requisite for understanding conflict. We must also uncover the nature and bases of social behavior; of the nature of social perception and social distance; of status, class, and power; of society and culture. Moreover, we must directly engage the nature of social conflict and violence.

This is done in *The Conflict Helix* (Rummel, 1976). There, social perception is described as a balance between the power of another to force perception on us and our own perspective. This balance is a *field of expression,* a totality of another's words, dress, gestures, and physical appearance, perceived within our psychological field. We give this field of expression unity by imputing to it causal structure, or by seeing it in terms of reasons or intentions. It is this field of expression toward which we behave, socially.

Social interaction comprises acts, actions, or practices that people mutually orient toward each other's selves. It is behavior that tries to influence or take into account another's subjective experiences or intentions, and such behavior is familistic, contractual, or compulsory.

The fields of expressions of socially interacting, mutually perceiving individuals, form a sociocultural field with these aspects. It is a complex of interdependent social interactions, a space of vehicles carrying meaning and values. It is a force field generated by man's goals and motives, attitudes and interests, sentiments and roles, and his will. It is a medium of sociocultural meanings, values, and norms. And it is the seat of field processes—the dynamic adjustments of interests called the conflict helix.

Of special importance is social distance as a field force, particularly the distance-components of status, power, and class. Status is a bundle of characteristics that are held to be desirable by consensus; it is a cluster of positive-valued aspects of a person's field of expression: his wealth, prestige, and power.

Power can be either social or nonsocial. In the latter case it is a vector toward manifestation, the assertive power of all beings toward identity, toward the manifestation of being. Social power is intentionally oriented toward another self, toward getting another to choose in certain ways. As Figure 1.2 indicates, there are six forms of social power: coercive, bargaining, intellectual, authoritative, altruistic, and manipulative.

Coercive and authoritative power underlie class distinctions, especially as seen through the concept of *antifield.* An antifield restrains, neutralizes or annihilates the free adjustment of individuals to field forces, and the most relevant type of antifield is the coercive organization. Through authoritative roles resting on coercive power, the social interaction between individuals in such an organization is regulated by command. Fields and antifields are opposites—as one advances, the other

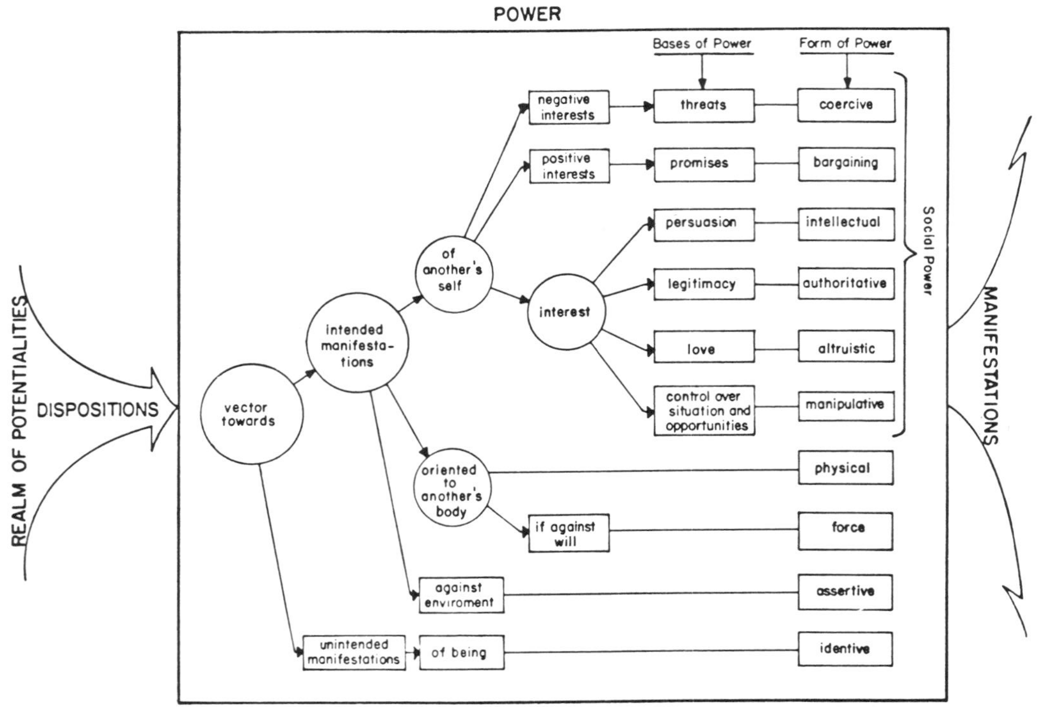
POWER
Bases of Power
Form of Power
REALM OF POTENTIALITIES
DISPOSITIONS
vector towards
intended manifesta-tions
of another's self
negative interests
positive interests
interest
threats
promises
persuasion
legitimacy
love
control over situation and opportunities
coercive
bargaining
intellectual
authoritative
altruistic
manipulative
Social Power
oriented to another's body
if against will
physical
force
against enviroment
assertive
unintended manifestations
of being
identive
MANIFESTATIONS

Figure 1.2

must recede. As coercion spreads, spontaneous interaction disappears.

There are two classes: those who command and those who obey, which is determined by the distribution of authoritative power in the coercive organization. Classes are thus dispositional conflict groups, delimiting the propensity to oppose or defend the status quo. They are reservoirs for interest groups and political parties.

Class struggle must become a political struggle. The state at any one time is an image of class conflict and balance, no less for socialist states run by the party elite and managers, than for capitalist ones.

The foregoing statements provide insight into conflict as a category and a process.

As a philosophical category, conflict is a *balancing of vectors of power.* It is the pushing and pulling, the giving and taking, the process of finding a balance between powers. Social conflict is then this confrontation of social powers; it is exclusively an aspect of social power.

Conflict consists of the levels of potentiality, dispositions, and manifestations. As potentiality, conflict is the space of all possible conflicts: the realm of potential opposing vectors of power, a *conflict-space.* As dispositions opposing each other within this space, conflict is a *structure.* As opposing powers and their indeterminate balancing, conflict is a *situation.*

Meanings, values, norms, status, and class are the common components of conflict-space, of potential conflict, and indeed, of man's *sociocultural space,* as shown in Figure 1.3. Potentiality becomes the actuality of opposing dispositions in the *structure of conflict.* Opposing dispositions are opposing attitudes that lie along the common components delineating man's similarities and dissimilarities. That is, cultural, status, and class distances are elements defining man's opposing dispositions. For dispositions to oppose, however, for there to be a structure of conflict, people must be aware of one another.

A *situation of conflict* is created by attitudes transformed into interests. Interests, which are vectors of power toward manifestation of a specific goal, are a necessary condition of a situation of conflict. Also involved in a situation of conflict are

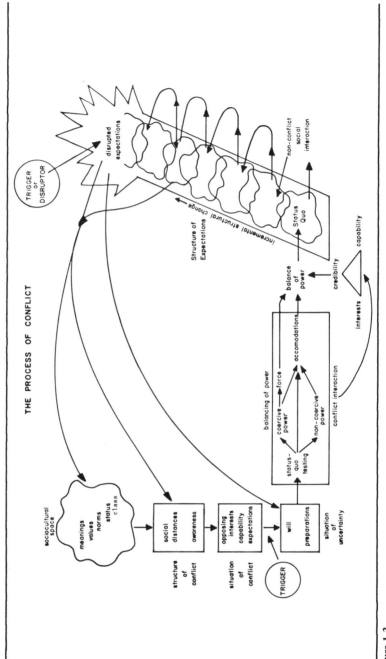

Figure 1.3

capabilities and expectations, particularly those defining the worth (credibility) of promises, threats, authority, expertise, love. Capability involves the resources a person has to manifest his interest. Together, *interest, credibility,* and *capability* define a situation of conflict.

A *balance of interests* is achieved in three ways: routinely within a structure of expectations, psychologically by the will inhibiting or transforming an interest to facilitate striving for self-esteem, and in conflict, by the will actively pursuing an interest in direct confrontation with other wills. In the latter case, there is balancing of interests manifesting conflict behavior. Such balancing is initiated by a *trigger* occasion that calls for a new structure of expectations, disrupts the prevailing structure, or serves as the last straw regarding expectations incongruent with current interests and capabilities. Therefore, the two major elements in balancing powers are will and trigger.

Once triggered, *conflict behavior* manifests acts, actions, or practices involved in the balancing of power. Such behavior is not necessarily violent, nor coercive, forceful, or antagonistic. Rather, conflict behavior mirrors the balancing of social power in its many forms, and it can be familistic and contractual, as well as antagonistic.

This confrontation between powers ends in accommodation—a *balance of power.* All social manifestations reflect either this balance or the antecedent balancing. The balance defines a *structure of expectations,* or social order—the rules, agreements, contracts, understandings, and so on, determined through the balancing of opposing powers. Society is interlaced by such orders, issued at various levels and segmented in diverse ways. It is the spontaneous outcome of these orders.

If left undisturbed, *social interaction* is an upward spiral of increasing order and stability, a *helix* (Figure 1.3). The balancing of power produces the structure of expectations, which is a balance among the interests, capabilities, and credibilities of the parties involved. Change in these elements, however, causes the structure of expectations to become increasingly incongruent with the underlying balance. This incongruence produces a strain toward rebalancing—toward conflict. Eventually the strain is such that a minor event can easily disrupt the structure and trigger a rebalancing. All interaction is either balancing—conflict behavior—or a cooperative interaction that reflects the structure of expectations.

The foregoing general view of social conflict introduces my primary concern, namely, collective conflict at the level of societies and states.

Societies are sociocultural fields or antifields. Generated by interests (powers), interconnected through the medium of meanings, values, and norms, laced by the forces of sociocultural distances and moved by the efforts of diverse wills, societies are multifold entities of different, overlapping intersecting, and nested structures of expectations. In other words, society is a complex of balances of power.

Three such complexes can be discriminated at the level of state-societies. One is the *authoritative society*, with a prevailing authoritative power based on legitimacy. A second is the *exchange society*, which is permeated by bargaining power and emphasizes rewards and promises. The third is the *coercive society*, an organization founded on threats and deprivation.

Regardless of type, each state-society has a political system that is a structure of expectations authoritatively governing the state. It may be characterized as open or closed, as allowing or controlling group autonomy, as normatively based, or past, present, or future oriented. These characteristics define a two-dimensional political space in which three types of political system—libertarian, authoritarian, and totalitarian—exist in a triangular relationship. This triangle can be further refined according to contemporary political formulas to locate on its anarchism, welfare liberalism, conservatism, fascism, and democratic socialism.

The political triangle (Figure 1.4) overlays society, where the communist and dynastic systems are the most prevalent manifestions of the totalitarian and authoritarian types, respectively. The different political systems are congruent with the different types of social system: exchange societies have libertarian systems, authoritative societies have authoritarian systems, and coercive societies have totalitarian systems.

All societies represent the outcome of the conflict process, comprise structures of expectations, and are built on multiple

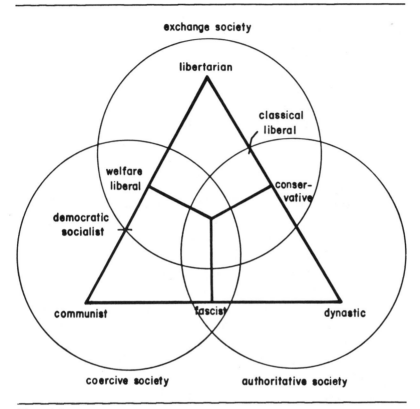

exchange society

libertarian

classical
liberal

welfare
liberal

conser-
vative

democratic
socialist

communist   fascist   dynastic

coercive society   authoritative society

Figure 1.4

and overlapping balances of powers among individuals. Thus we can draw the following general propositions for conflict and violence at the level of societies:

(1) *Aggregate conflict manifestations are random* across societies in relation to their specific structures of expectations.

(2) *Change produces conflict,* namely, the change that alters power relationships promotes conflict, and the change from one society (power configuration) to another type involves the most violence; as the change (rate) in education and communication increases relative to economic development, the probability of conflict also grows. Therefore, the ratio of the growth

in social consciousness in society to its development provides a measure of the rigidity of the status quo and the likelihood of conflict.

(3) *Power shapes conflict.* All modern states are antifields to some extent, and the front between antifield and social field is the region of potential social storms. Across societies there is a curvilinear relationship between elite force and manifest conflict.

(4) *There are three dimensions of conflict,* each associated with a particular type of state-society.

(5) *Exchange societies manifest pluralistic conflicts* or turmoil, such as riots and demonstrations, and conflict behavior generally involves relatively isolated groups, events, or issues. Conflict may occasionally reach the level of societies, but the freedom to remove political elites and influence public policy, and the conflict-defusing function of competitive political parties, provide mechanisms for bargaining and compromise far short of revolutionary violence. Moreover, multiple group and class memberships create cross-pressures inhibiting the formation of a conflict front across the entire society.

(6) *Authoritative societies manifest communal/traditional conflict.* The major divisions traversing these societies are communal, often based on homogeneity of race, language, and tribal membership, as well as territorial separation. Where communal activities are left alone by the state, conflict is minimal. But where authoritarian rulers try to extend their legitimacy over such communities, communal violence is often the result. This conflict is exascerbated if racial-language-tribal cleavages are also the line of class divisions.

(7) *Coercive societies manifest elite violence.* In coercive societies conflict is manifested by class terror and repression, and by elite purges. Coercive societies are the most violent, being responsible for more deaths than occurred in the two world wars.

1.2 PERSPECTIVES

Some for renown, on scraps of learning dote,
And think they grow immortal as they quote.

Edward Young, *Love of Fame*

In sum, the social field is a continuum of latent meanings, values, norms, statuses, and classes. It is the seat of social powers. Man strives to manifest these powers through others to gratify his interests and his superordinate goal. Powers meet, conflict, balance, and conflict again. The field is alive. The process of conflict—the conflict helix—is a dynamic swirl of manifest activity and latent potentialities and dispositions, but with an order and direction.

This is the most abstract understanding of the social field and conflict. It constitutes a perspective on the social "things-in-themselves" that underlie social phenomena. It deals with categories of the understanding essential for cognitively organizing these phenomena, with the most fundamental perspective on man in society, with an ontology of conflict.

But this comprehension of social conflict is unfamiliar to most social scientists; indeed, most will be unsympathetic to an approach less concerned with empirical patterns and dependencies than with their latent aspects, which we can never know concretely. Indeed, after working through the previous volumes (Rummel, 1975, 1976), the reader may ask with some exasperation: What about aggression or frustration-aggression? What about relative deprivation? What about misperception, tension, hostility, and stereotyping? What about poverty, inequality, and exploitation? What about competition and cross-pressures? What about anomie, the conflict of values, and change? What about the processes of conflict proposed by Sorokin, Coleman, and others? What about violence in the form of war or revolution? And the more philosophical may ask: What about the conflict of opposites? What about fate or cause and effect? What about the inevitability of conflict?

These important questions are considered in the following chapters. For the power of the field perspective can best be seen and understood in its ability to encompass, clarify, or confront prevailing scientific and common-sense views on conflict. But to deal with these questions imposes a burden. The literature on conflict and violence is vast. The approaches, views, and conclusions are varied, contrasting, and often contradictory. Yet I must encompass this literature, whether it deals with war, riots, strikes, family quarrels, juvenile delinquency, gangs, politics, assassinations, or revolutions; whether the approach be anthropological, sociological, economic, philosophical, or political; whether the method be historical, descriptive, philosophical, or quantitative.

To demonstrate that the conflict helix underlies all conflict, we must deal with concrete conflict as seen through man's many perspectives. To do this comprehensively, however, requires summarizing various views and approaches within a direction. My interest is less in presenting a view of conflict, such as frustration-aggression, than in sketching the view sufficiently to show its relationship to or contradiction of the conflict helix. Thus certain favorite theories or views inevitably receive less discussion than some would wish, and certain faddish explanations of conflict are only mentioned in passing.

Three perspectives dominate theories and explanations of conflict, and these serve to organize my discussion. *The first perspective is on man, himself, psychologically.* The explanation for conflict, its source or causes, lies in man's nature, psychological processes, or attributes. Thus man conflicts because he is aggressive, frustrated, insecure, altruistic, or selfish; because of his status or poverty; because of his learning, ignorance, or culture; because of his misperception, misunderstanding, or stereotypes; because of incongruence.

The second perspective is on man, sociologically. He conflicts because of the social situation, the context within which he finds himself. Here conflict is understood as an aspect of cooperation and differentiation, as a result of nonsegmented pressures, overpopulation, or the lack of external threats. It is due to social distance, class, contact, relative power, or inequality; to inconsistent values or norms. This perspective includes the dispute between the functional and conflict models of man, and the Classical Liberal and Marxists views of conflict and the contemporary revisions of von Mises, Dahrendorf, and

Rex. This perspective also includes the view that conflict is simply a manifestation (or instrument) of change; it reflects a transition period between cultural types or a breakdown in crystallized values and norms; it constitutes a set of phases of crystallizing and disintegrating congruences between expectations and gratifications; it is a political process through which a status quo is tested and altered; or it constitutes a cyclic phenomenon.

The third perspective is philosophical: conflict is seen as the incessant and natural clash of opposites, determined and inevitable. The normative implications of conflict can be viewed from this perspective, especially regarding social justice.

Of course the psychological, sociological, and philosophical perspectives are an idealization of the literature, since the same explanation may cross perspectives and mix levels. Generally, however, we can locate a view as being more in one of these perspectives than another, and I do this in the following chapters.

One final introductory comment. My intention is not to present a bibliographic review of this literature, but an intellectual synthesis in relation to the conflict helix. I refer to particular works for purposes of clarification or exemplification, or because they are central to various views on conflict. If favored works are slighted, I trust their major ideas have been encompassed in the discussion nonetheless.

1.3 SUMMARY

Conflict in Psychological Perspective

(1) *Aggression.* Aggression is a disposition, power, or manifestation characterized by assault, attack, invasion. The core notion is of a forceful setting upon, either as tendency or behavior. In social relations it is a disposition toward or a manifesting of interests offensively, and it is woven into the process of conflict. Aggression does not cause conflict; it innately characterizes the manifesting process. Aggressive needs add fuel to the process, aggressive attitudes add substance, aggressive temperaments add style. Regardless of source, however, aggression is a manifestation within a conflict process.

(2) *Frustration-aggression.* Frustration is neither a necessary nor a sufficient cause of aggression.

(3) *Relative deprivations.* For an understanding of conflict, relative deprivation is most appropriately understood as a sense of injustice in comparison with others. This sense of injustice fundamentally defines the class consciousness necessary to the class struggle within all organizations, including the state.

(4) *Misperception.* Misperceptions may underlie conflict, which then can be seen as a means for correcting the misperceptions or enabling people to live with them. Manifest conflict, however, also can result from a real opposition of interests and correct perceptions.

(5) *Cognitive dissonance.* Dissonance operates as part of the conflict helix in its social significance. It may create opposing interests and provoke their balancing, and it may be rectified by the resulting conflict. However conflict is also manifest without dissonance.

(6) *Expectations.* Although the expectation of conflict can contribute to its inception, expectations do not create opposing interest, nor do they necessarily influence the perception of other's capability and credibility. These other aspects discipline and limit the effect of expectations on the occurrence of conflict.

(7) *Righteousness.* Our feelings about how men ought to be treated are basic to understanding conflict and violence on the level of societies. A central ingredient in the class struggle, righteousness provides an explanation for the appeal of a political formula. Such moral conflicts have been the most bitter and violent in man's history.

Conflict in Sociological Perspective

(1) *Marxism.* Marx's emphasis on conflict, classes and their relations to the state, and social change, is a powerful perspective shared by the conflict helix.

(2) *Cross-pressures.* The presence in society of multiple groups, interests, classes, and statuses guarantees the existence of a constant level of conflict across society, but also ensures that the intensity and scope of conflict will be limited. Freedom for the individual assures the development of conflict-limiting cross-pressures.

(3) *Overpopulation.* Density is generally unrelated to conflict. Its importance depends on the meanings, values, and norms associated with the number of people present. Crucial is the subjective significance of density, and this is a matter of culture and related structures of expectations.

(4) *Anomie.* Anomie is a condition of an incongruent structure of expectations, primed for a trigger provoking manifest conflict and the creation of a new structure. Extensive crime and disorder, extensive disobedience and "immoral" behavior, are signs that the societal consensus—the societal structure of expectations—is inadequate.

(5) *Similarity and dissimilarity.* What similarity and dissimilarity between individuals, relevant to their conflict, are measured by their distance vectors on the common components of sociocultural space? These are differences in language, religion-philosophy, ethics-law, science, fine arts, wealth, power, prestige, and class. Differences in attitudes and interests lie along these distance vectors, and the concordance in norms between individuals in interaction is a function of their structure of expectations. Antagonism will be generated between men as they are distant in their expectations and interests. However the overt expression of this antagonism depends on the conflict process.

(6) *Change.* The perspective on conflict as a helix is a dynamic view that is related to the process theories of Sorokin, Marx, Chalmers Johnson, and Lewis Fry Richardson. Change affects conflict insofar as change promotes an incongruence between underlying interests, credibilities, and capabilities, and the structure of expectations. The breakdown in such expectations and their restructuring through conflict is the universal adjustment to change.

Conflict in Philosophical Perspective

(1) *The conflict of opposites.* The conflict helix—the process of balancing, balance, disruption, and balancing—is a unity of opposites through which society changes and evolves. Conflict transforms itself into harmony, and harmony into conflict; war into peace, and peace into war. Both are aspects of the same process, an inseparable unity in the field of man.

(2) *Determinism.* The same social phenomenon can be viewed as either free or determined. Located in the phenomenological realm, an event is determined by the process of conflict; as a manifestation of man's underlying reason and will, however, it reflects man's freedom. Whether we see an action as free or determined depends on our intentions as social scientists. If our interest is in the moral aspects of the process, in what ought to be in the future, in what man can create through such a process, then we can emphasize man's underlying freedom.

(3) *Inevitability.* Is conflict inevitable? Yes, insofar as social man must establish a balance with others, for conflict is the process for doing so. Moreover, man cannot escape coercion, thus coercive conflict; but he can determine its scope, amount, and direction through the society that he creates.

(4) *The inevitability of violence.* A basic motive of collective violence is altruistic or fraternal, it is concern for our fellow man. But the occurrence of violence is due to a crisis of legitimacy, an ambiguity of coercive power between contending groups, and a weakening of credibility. It is a product of change and is shaped by power. Some violence in society is inevitable, although its scope and intensity varies among societies. Exchange societies have the least violence; coercive the most.

(5) *And intentional humanism: the view of conflict as a helix is consistent with an ethics that sees man as free, creative, responsible, and teleological.* Indeed, the helix is the sociological plane of intentional humanism, as the dynamic psychological field is its psychological plane.

(6) *Freedom, social justice, and conflict.* These are interdependent; in the final analysis they must be considered *together* for an understanding of conflict, of freedom, or of social justice.

  (a) *Freedom as the highest value.* Only the individual can decide for himself his interests, costs, and ethical constraints.

  (b) *Social justice is the balance of powers.* Justice is an individual question, not a societal one. To impose justice through the state in terms of what is best for society, or ultimately good or bad, right or wrong, is to impose the definition of justice by a few on all others.

(c) *Social justice is maximal freedom.* If justice lies in individual interests, morality, and calculation of costs, then the more freedom man has, the more social justice.

(d) *Maximal freedom will minimize violence and extreme conflict.* Freedom creates diversity, overlapping group memberships, and crosscutting interests, ties, and classes. This segments conflict and drains it off before a conflict front can form across the entire society.

(e) *Maximal freedom will check and balance the aggrandizement of coercive power.* If diversity is enabled to develop and individuals are free to strike their own balances, opposition based on differing interests will curb aggrandizing power.

(f) *The ultimate solution to violent conflict is freedom and decentralization of state power.*

PART I

CONFLICT IN PSYCHOLOGICAL PERSPECTIVE

The adventurer is within us, and he contends for our favour with the social man we are obliged to be. These two sorts of life are incompatible; one we hanker after, the other we are obliged to. There is no other conflict so deep and bitter as this.

William Bolitho, Introduction to
Twelve Against the Gods

Chapter 2

AGGRESSION

Aggression: (1) An unprovoked attack; the first attack in a quarrel; an assault, an inroad. (2) The practice of setting upon anyone; the making of an attack or assault.

Oxford English Dictionary

For an understanding of conflict, hostility, and violence, many have looked to inner man. Some have observed that by nature, by instinct, by heredity, man aggresses on his fellows. His conflict is phylogenetic in origin, and violence is part of his nature. Others have qualified this, asserting that aggression is only a potentiality manifested through a particular psychological structure and processes. Or, admitting that heredity provides the possibility, still others see conflict, aggression, and violence as the outcome of blocked drives, needs, desires—that is, of frustration.

Many of these views coalesce around the question of aggression. Is aggression instinctual or learned? Is it an appetitive drive or an instrumental action? A character syndrome or a cultural manifestation? By an answer, it is believed that we can resolve the why of man's social conflict, violence, and war. Therefore, I deal first with the general issue of aggression, summarizing the major approaches and relating these to the conflict helix. I then focus on the particular frustration-aggression theory, which has so excited contemporary social scientists.

2.1 APPROACHES TO AGGRESSION

In general we can identify five approaches to understanding man's aggression: ethological, psychotherapeutic, social learning, frustration-aggression, and cultural. The biological approach seeks the sources of aggression in man's phylogenetic nature, mainly through the ethological study of man as a member of the animal kingdom. The major scientist associated with this approach is Konrad Lorenz, the author of *On Aggression* (1966), which helped bring back to respectability the instinctual view of man,[1] popularized ethology,[2] and spawned a counterliterature on aggression.[3] In sum, for Lorenz aggression is a "driving power," an instinct toward the preservation of life, thus species. It underlies all kinds of behavior that on the surface have nothing to do with aggression and functions not only to preserve but to evenly distribute a species over the environment, to select the strongest, and to protect the young.

Lorenz clearly adopts a hydraulic model of aggression. Within animals, including man, aggressive energy accumulates like the buildup of a need for sex or food. If blocked, this energy may be redirected to substitute objects, or it may explode on those nearby. If no adequate aggression-releasing stimulus is at hand, one will be actively sought. Aggression thus comes from within. Man does not learn to be aggressive. He is born to be aggressive.

Lorenz believes that species develop a number of mechanisms for redirecting or inhibiting intraspecific aggression. Ritualized fighting in which no animal is really hurt drains off aggression, and submissive behavior can block it. Carnivorous creatures, especially, with their ability to kill easily, have developed rituals and inhibitions limiting and formalizing intraspecific aggression. Man, however, does not belong to the order of carnivores and has not developed such a protective mechanism. But he has unbalanced nature; through the development of his technology of weapons, he has far exceeded the killing power of any carnivore, but has no counterbalancing inhibitions. Thus man is a great danger to himself. Undeterred by the submission of others, unlimited within any fighting ritual, he releases his instinctual aggression on his fellow man. Aggression, nature's species-preserving drive, through man's weapons has become species destroying.

Lorenz sees three ways to help avoid aggression. We must first know outselves, especially through ethology and psychoanalysis. Self-knowledge will help us devise mechanisms for redirecting aggression. Second, we must promote friendships across group lines, since bonds developed between diverse people aid in inhibiting mutual aggression. Third, and most important, we must channel aggression onto substitute objects or into aggression-draining activities, such as sports and athletic competition.

Although for many social scientists the name of Lorenz is synonymous with the ethological position on aggression, his ethological data and inferences are strongly disputed by his colleagues[4] among whom the consensus is that aggression is neither wholly instinctual nor learned, but the outcome of an interaction between an animal's disposition, environment, and social structure. And social structure often appears to be the key to understanding the more violent forms of aggression.

> ... social organization is not something which is born into an animal, but something which is developed, and if social organization is disturbed, harmless or even beneficial aggressive behavior can be transformed into destructive violence. Thus the violent baboons in the London Zoo studied by Zuckerman were a group of individuals strange to each other and hence a disorganized society. The undisturbed societies of baboons studied by Washburn and DeVore on the South African plains present an entirely different picture. Fighting is present but controlled by a dominance order, and is chiefly directed against predators, and one sees the baboons risking their lives for the benefit of a group. Thus a baboon, in common with many other mammals, has the capacity to develop destructive violence under conditions of social disorganization, whereas under the proper conditions of social organization he has the capacity to develop peaceful and cooperative behavior, to direct fighting into useful channels, and to act in a manner which might well be described as altruistic. One wonders whether the same might not be said of man. [Scott, 1973:139]

Animals, including man, develop a social structure mediating between their needs and the environment. Even territoriality, often considered to be instinctual, reflects social structure.[5] If this structure is disrupted, and animals must adjust to new situations such as crowding,[6] radical change of environment, or scarcity of food, aggression is most manifest. That is, *the conflict helix appears as a general process underlying aggression among many kinds of animals.*

The various schools of psychotherapy represent a second approach to aggression. Whether an aggressive drive is or is not instinctual, such behavior is seen as an outcome of underlying psychological structures, processes, and mechanisms. Aggression is an aspect of man's totality, his genetic inheritance, his biophysiological constitution and chemiconeurological state, and his psychology. The sources lie in man, but unlike the phylogenetically programmed single instinct of Lorenz, aggression manifests a particular configuration of biological and psychological elements, only one of which may be instinctual.

The first psychotherapist to propose an aggressive drive was Alfred Adler. In 1908 he published[7] his theory that aggression is a superordinate drive that dominates motor behavior and consciousness and is a confluence of other drives. It is innate, the organizing principle of man's activities, and (of greatest significance to the psychotherapist) can turn on the self, creating various pathological manifestations.

Adler soon reinterpreted this drive as a masculine protest (a drive to compensate for feelings of inferiority), and finally as an upward striving for completion or perfection. In this later view, man was driven, above all else, to improve himself, to overcome. Aggression then became subordinate to this drive, and indeed, when directed at society, was a pathological form of striving.

Although eclipsed by the work of Freud and almost forgotten for decades, many of Adler's views[8] have been revived and transformed. One such transformation is manifested through existential psychotherapy, as in the work of Rollo May.

May's major analysis dealing with aggression is *Power and Innocence* (1972). He considers power to be man's basic drive and aggression as one form of this drive. Power has five ontological levels for May (1972:40-42): first, simply the power to be, to exist, to assert oneself as a living thing, akin to what I have elsewhere called identive power (Rummel, 1976, Section 19.4); second, the power of self-affirmation, to be recognized and to become significant; third, the power of self-assertion, of pushing against opposition; fourth, aggression, the application of power to overcome blocked self-assertion; and fifth, violence, to which man resorts when nonviolent aggression is fruitless.

Aggression is basic to man, but culturally formed. Not all bad, it is a way the individual affirms and asserts himself. It is manifested, for example, in initiating a relationship, in trying to penetrate another's consciousness, in warding off threatening powers, and in love-making. "The truth is that practically everything we do is a mixture of positive and negative forms of aggression" (May, 1972:152). The expression of power in its aggressive, constructive forms is healthy. It is when such expression is inhibited or blocked that violence occurs. Violence expresses impotence.[9]

The views of Adler and modern neo-Adlerians stand in marked contrast to psychoanalytic thought. Adler was a member of Freud's psychoanalytic school when he proposed his aggressive drive in 1908. Freud initially rejected this view, believing that aggression did not constitute any special instinct or drive (Ansbacher and Ansbacher, 1956:37). It was not until more than a decade later that Freud, perhaps as a result of the bitter experiences of World War I and its aftermath, recognized an aggressive instinct. This he first elaborated in *Beyond the Pleasure Principle,* developing the concept in his later works.[10]

In Freud's earlier theory, man was dominated by self-preservation and sexual instincts (the ego instinct and eros). Aggression had no status as a separate instinct but was a component part of eros—an aspect of his sexuality. Moreover, eros was a tension-releasing instinct. As in the hydraulic model of aggression, man builds up internal tension that must be divested. Release (catharsis) constitutes pleasure. This was a mechanical conception, reflecting Freud's early psychophysical and mechanistic perspective.

In moving to the fore the idea of a death instinct, Freud developed a particularly biological conception. All living things were now driven by two competing instincts. One was a life instinct (still eros) driving to create, maintain, and unify living things into larger systems. The death instinct drives toward breaking up living systems and dissolving them into quiescence.

Being the ultimate application of the pleasure principle, death is the divestiture of all tension, the perfect state.

The death instinct is directed inward toward extinguishing the organism. To preserve the organism, the libido does battle with the death instinct and directs it outward, whereupon it becomes external aggression, the drive for mastery, the will to power. Aggression is therefore secondary, a deflection of the death instinct away from the self. Moreover, in its battle with the libido, the death instinct may combine with eros into sadism or masochism, two of its worst common pathological manifestations.

To Freud, then, aggression was always negative or destructive. It was antilife or pathological. And behavior was a manifestation either of eros, of the desire for death, or of a combination of these. The striving for identity, for self-assertion, for social interest, had no role in Freud's perspective.

Psychoanalysis has been an influential approach and framework for understanding man's behavior, and the social sciences have been enriched by it. But it is such concepts as eros, libido, ego, id, superego, and catharsis that have been found useful. Few have accepted the idea of a death instinct, even though some of Freud's successors, such as Melanie Klein (1950), have adopted and developed this view.

A recent work on aggression by the psychoanalyst Erich Fromm (1973) revises the notion of the death instinct in a direction consistent with current ethological findings and psychological research. Freud saw aggression as rooted in a death instinct, although its manifestation may blend with eros. Fromm, however, recognizes two independent sources, only one of which is instinctual. Instinctual aggression is benign and defensive; uninstinctual aggression, rooted in man's character, is malignant and destructive.

According to Fromm, man instinctually protects himself against threats to his survival, his freedom (1973:198-199), and other basic values. Harm or destructiveness that results from this defense is unintended or purely instrumental. The aim is to overcome threat, the activity ends when the threat does. Thus benign aggression is reactive, not appetitive. It is aroused by stimuli, not internally generated by an increase in tension. In this Fromm's instinctual aggression differs fundamentally from that of Lorenz and Freud.

Moreover, where human aggression for Lorenz and Freud is largely negative, hostile, and destructive, for Fromm instinctual aggression is positive, contributing to man's growth, self-assertion, and independence, and to the survival of the species.

Malignant aggression, however, results from specifically human passions seated in our character. Man's organic needs and emotions are integrated and organized according to his major goals.[11] This structure of organization is his character. It is a "human phenomenon" (1973:253)[12] enabling man to adapt to multiple environments and challenges.

Character structures differ, and malignant aggression, organized as it is within specific structures, may never be manifested. Moreover, it takes different forms. It can be vengeful or ecstatic hate and destructiveness. It can be sadistic, with the desire to have absolute control over others, or masochistic in wanting to be completely under another's control. It can be a passion to destroy and tear apart living things. Such forms are social categories resulting from man's history and institutions. For Fromm, the way to reduce malignant aggression is to radically alter "techno-cybernetic society," to create new forms of decentralization in which man would be freer to assert his self and live the good life.[13]

Not all psychotherapists fall within the schools mentioned. Some, like Anthony Storr (1968), adopt almost completely Lorenz's instinctual view and hydraulic model of aggression, adding to it various psychological mechanisms that inhibit or channel its expression. Storr feels that aggression is an essential element in society, encouraging competition for food and sex, and ensuring peace and order through status hierarchies. Since it is instinctual, it is "impossible to believe that there could ever be a society without strife and competition" (p. 53). Moreover, aggression is not all negative. In childhood it is a drive toward the eventual independence and separation from the parents. Indeed, as an adult, the more dependent a person, the more latent the aggression (p. 44).

Aggression is also a means by which people establish their identity. Identity requires opposition, which is manifested through aggression. The negative effect of aggression is due to confusion between it and paranoid hostility or hatred (in which frustration plays a large role). Such hostility is reduced by encouraging competition (to drain it off), diminishing over-population, and preventing aggression from turning into hate.

The psychotherapeutic perspectives that have been reviewed constitute the major ones in which aggression plays an important role.[14] In sum, they all include some form of aggression whether internally based, seated in man's phylo-genetic nature, or rooted in his subconscious drives and needs. They differ from the ethological approach of Lorenz in emphasizing the particularly human organization, psychological processes, and mechanisms involved. They include the *person,* the psyche with its own laws.

A contrasting approach to aggression is provided by social learning theory (Rotter, 1954, Mowrer, 1950, Bandura, 1973). As in the instinctualism of some ethologists, the person is omitted. But rather than being an innate drive in search of gratification, aggression is said to be acquired through experi-ence, behavioral models, and reward and punishment.

This is not to deny man's inherited neurophysiological and phylogenetic potentiality to aggress. The learning theorist recognizes this, but argues that actualization is dependent on external influences, on the causal nexus between stimuli, consequences, and reinforcement. The shift is from internal instincts or drives to external causes and conditions.

The basic focus is on aggression as socially defined[15] injurious or destructive behavior. Then we must determine how such behavior is acquired, instigated, maintained, and modified. Man learns to be aggressive when such behavior enables him to satisfy his wants or desires, when others' aggression is perceived (through movies or television, say) to be rewarded, and when alternative nonaggressive behavior is less successful. Man soon realizes that strong assertiveness pays, that "the squeaky wheel gets the oil." Once learned, and reinforced through social approval and acquired status, through the esteem and pride of success, and through observing the success of others, aggression will be avoided only if it becomes risky, if costs in punishment or negative sanctions develop and nonaggressive behavioral alternatives are rewarded (Bandura, 1973:222).

This theory of aggression is fundamentally behavioral. There is concern about goals and intentions, but the focus is on stimulus-response, on observable response contingent experiences, on patterns of reinforcement. Laboratory experiments provide the research setting, and the findings emerge from the quantitative analysis of observed and systematized data. In this they differ from the naturalistic observations of instinctualists and the case-intuitive *verstehen* approach of psychotherapists.

This behavioral approach is shared by those espousing what is perhaps the dominant view of aggression today, namely, that aggression is a consequence of man's frustrated goals, desires, needs, or drives.[16] The intensity with which a goal is desired, the degree to which frustration blocks this desire, and the history of an individual's frustration presumably predict the amount of his aggression.

Frustration-aggression theory has a dominant role in many social programs. Deprivations, inequalities, and exploitation are believed to frustrate the desires of the poor and disadvantaged. Delinquency, crime, rioting, and the high level of interpersonal aggression among some minority groups are believed to result from such frustrations. The solution thus appears clear: extensive social service and welfare programs to overcome these frustrations in the short run, and in the long run, a comprehensive institutional change to promote social equality and justice.

Because of the contemporary popularity and significance of frustration-aggression theory, I treat it separately in a subsequent chapter, along with its variants, such as the theory of relative deprivation.

There is one final approach to consider, that of the cultural anthropologists such as Alexander Alland, Jr. (1972). Aggression is seated within a culture; it is learned in the same way a language is learned. To understand it, the research should focus on the cultural context of aggression and its function in the maintenance and development of the culture.

The basic observation is that some cultures are relatively free of collective aggression and seldom manifest interpersonal violence and destructiveness.[17] Therefore, although man has the potentiality for aggressive behavior, whether it is manifest is a matter of cultural learning. Man is not aggressive. Cultures are aggressive.

Clearly, the cultural approach shares with social learning theory the emphasis on the external sources—on learning. They differ in methodology, one centering on quantitative laboratory experimentation, the other on the naturalistic observation and absorption of cultures. They differ also on the focus. Learning theory emphasizes that which impinges on the individual. It is individual centered, stressing the development of aggression as an interaction between response, reinforcement, stimuli, and so forth. The cultural approach, however, is less concerned with the individual and some determinate variables than with the total field of norms, meanings, and values within which certain behavioral patterns develop.

In sum, I have identified five general approaches to or theories of aggression. Aggression results from an instinct shared with all animals, from an instinct or drive manifested through particularly human, subconscious, psychological mechanisms and processes, from an acquired response pattern, from frustrated goals or drives, or from cultural learning. More generally these approaches see aggression as resulting from man's instincts or drives, from environmental influences, or some combination. Aggression is inherited or learned or both.

To try to understand how field theory, particularly the conflict helix, relates to these theories, I must focus first on aggression itself.

2.2 THE NATURE OF AGGRESSION

A survey of the literature indicates the many different senses in which "aggression" is used. Like the concept of power, aggression has many forms. It can mean causing another injury or creating destruction, attacking another, or simply engaging in fighting. It can refer to strong, assertive behavior (an aggressive lover) or an offensive-besetting manner (as aggressive salesman). It can refer to a disposition (an aggressive personality) or an action. It can mean an emotional state (anger or hostility) or an intention (to hurt someone). It can be self-assertive, or sado-masochistic. It can be instrumental or ritualistic, playful or spontaneous. It can be benign or malignant, positive or negative. Aggression, in short, is many things. It is, like so many of our crucial social concepts, a dialectical term to be contextually worked, a sense to be created within a perspective.

No wonder, then, that the asserted causes and cures of aggression vary so remarkably. It is caused by frustration or social arrangements and culture. It is instinctual or pathological. It results from threats to freedom or vital interests. It originates in wounded narcissism or a blocked death instinct. It is produced by dependency or impotence. It is engendered by low self-esteem or blocked self-assertion. It is born out of weak bonds or violated norms. It is inspired by role models.

And the cures? Man must develop new forms of decentralized institutions or eliminate some crowding. He must reduce paranoid hostility or promote friendship. He must expand his self-knowledge or encourage self-expression. He must release tension through sport or find vicarious outlets. He must reward nonaggression and punish aggression. He must satisfy his needs.

From such variance in meaning and posited causes and cures, it should be clear that our view of aggression has considerable latitude. Facts are insufficient, *for what must be resolved first is the orientation toward phenomena that will determine the factual angle and range.* Moreover, as has been my refrain throughout, we must weigh the ethical nature of our perspective, consider the social consequences of a perspective we may hold. *Where we have many degrees of freedom in choosing our view, as we do on aggression, let us choose in the direction of man's freedom, creativity, and dignity.*

What then is aggression, within the perspective of the social field and intentional humanism? Within a framework of social potentialities, dispositions, powers, and manifestations? First, aggression is ontologically a manner or style of becoming—*it is disposed to be, becoming, or being offensive;* that is, a disposition, power, or manifestation characterized by assault, attack, invasion. The core notion is of a forceful setting upon, either as tendency or behavior. The antonym of aggression is defensiveness, which is being protective and reactive.

To assault or attack does not necessarily mean to engage in physical or violent action, for we can cast an aggressive eye at a party, invade a person's quiet, or attack another verbally without threatening or inflicting physical harm or injury. Social scientists tend to see aggression as murder, fighting, war, and hitting as the many possible kinds of violence and destructiveness. Equating such behavior with aggression misses the subjective nature of aggression and focuses on physical characteristics that apply only to some forms of aggression in some cultures. A raised eyebrow, a deliberately missed appointment, or a stare can be more aggressive in some cultures than a violent shove in others.

Moreover, defining aggression by objective behavior (or a tendency toward such) ignores the two-sidedness of violence. One can beset another with violence, or violence can be used to defend oneself. Is the man who attacks and fights off a thug aggressive? Is the nation that defends its borders against invasion aggressive? Is the girl who kicks a rapist in the groin aggressive? Of course not. Yet, most definitions of aggression equate all acts of violence, defensive and otherwise. To be aggressive is to be offensive. No particular kind of behavior or power is meant. Aggression is a style. It can permeate all a person's behavior, or it can color none.

With this understanding, I can now relate aggression to power in its various forms. In *The Conflict Helix* (Chapter 19) I point out that power—a vector toward manifestation, a pushing toward completion, specificity, determinateness—has many forms. There is identive power—the unintended manifestation of being. An aspect of existing, and confronting the powers of nature, identive power can be aggressive. We can imagine an aggressive storm that unleashes its fury, an aggressive shark that tears apart a swimmer, an aggressive dog that chases anything that moves, or an aggressive child who disrupts a household. This is *identive aggression,* the offensive setting upon the environment as part of being. Not all things assail or attack reality with their power. A chair, a pebble, a path are passive, defensive. Their power declares their identity, confronts other powers, but does not push outward and invade the being of others.

Identive aggression is a part of interpersonal relations. Unintended, it is not social. It is personal, a thrusting power of physique, character, or behavior; a style in which nature's multifold actualities are unconsciously realized. Thus we speak of aggressive beauty, dominating personality, or besetting behavior.

Aggression, however, may be intended. We may purposely act in an aggressive manner toward others physically, toward their selves, or toward the environment. Intended power directed toward the environment is assertive. If such power is offensive, an attacking of one's surroundings, it is *assertive aggression.* It is a form of self-assertion, a purposive expression of self. A boy walking through the fields happily hacking off flowers with a stick is assertive in this manner, as is the hunter tracking deer or the person smashing an outworn desk with a sledge hammer to make kindling. The fundamental notion is of attacking the environment intentionally.

Most often self-assertion is thought of in terms of asserting oneself against others, either as putting up a vigorous defense, expressing one's interests, or opposing the invasion of one's rights. The term also has the positive meaning of "making a dent," of confronting and overcoming, of pushing against and forward. All these meanings represent different forms of power, which I have tried to distinguish in the previous volume (Rummel, 1976, Chapter 20). In addition, assertion may be offensive or defensive. To label all self-assertion a type of aggression (whether called benign or positive) is to confuse the grim, willful determination of a lone survivor in a lifeboat at sea—displaying a passive form of self-assertion—with the aggressive assertion of a man chopping down a tree.

Assertive aggression is offensive power intentionally directed toward man's environment. Another form of power, thus of aggression, is intentionally directed toward another's body. This is force, the use of physical power to manifest one's interests against another. The other's self is ignored, indeed, force is applied to achieve some purpose in spite of or over the opposition of the other self. *Forceful aggression,* which usually involves violence but not necessarily injury to another, is the offensive use of force. For example, Germany's attack on Poland in 1939, Japan's attack on Pearl Harbor in 1941, and North Korea's attack on South Korea in 1950 were forceful acts of aggression. The guerrilla band that attacks a police station or the police forces that attack demonstrators with clubs are using aggressive force.

Force, however, also may be nonaggressive. It may be defensive, as when a nation resists invasion, as the Soviet Union did in 1941-1943. Also acting defensively is the storekeeper who rigs the back door of his store with a booby trap to prevent theft or vandalism.

Not all force, therefore, is aggressive. Some mistakenly equate force, fighting, and violence with aggression, but this is to ignore the positive and protective uses of force—for example, to defend a person's freedom, independence, and deep, personal values against others.

So far, I have considered only nonsocial aggression that is directed unconsciously or intentionally against the environment or others' bodies. Social power is a vector toward manifestation through another self, of which there are six forms: coercive, bargaining, intellectual, authoritative, altruistic, and manipulative. Each form can be offensive or defensive; each can be an invasive, thrusting power, or a reactive, defensive opposition. Let us consider *coercive aggression* first.

Coercion is the use of threats or deprivations to induce another to do what he would otherwise not do. The physical violence used is instrumental in pressuring another's will to yield. He who initially attacks another physically or with threats is coercively aggressive if this behavior is directed at another's self. But coercion also can be defensive, as when a child threatens to scream if spanked, a popular president threatens to resign if the military intervene in politics, or a nation threatens nuclear retaliation against the cities of a possible attacker.

Coercion emphasizes threats or deprivations. Bargaining power, on the other hand, is manifested through promising rewards to another self. Bargaining power can be aggressive. Here we have social aggression not characterized by physical force or violence, although it has the same core meaning as the most aggressive destructiveness—that is, to set upon, to assail or assault, to attack another. We all have experienced this kind of *aggressive bargaining,* whether from a door-to-door vacuum cleaner salesman or from a hawker at a county fair.

Intellectual power, the use of expertise or persuasion to manifest one's interest through another self, is clearly aggressive in the attack on the ideas or competence of another, or in the invasion of another's beliefs with an army of facts and arguments marshalled to change the other's notions. Such is the *intellectual aggression* of the missionary, the dogmatic and outspoken scholar, or the "expert" who makes a career out of besetting others with the virtues of a single technique.

Authoritative power appeals to our concepts of what is right, proper, correct—legitimate. This is the power of the public official, of the judge, of the bishop, of the boss in any occupational hierarchy, to have others do what he wants by virtue of his position. And authoritative power can be aggressive: witness the police who invade a citizen's home to search for narcotics, the secret police who forcibly remove a suspect to an interrogation center, or the "hanging judge" who with all the sanctions at his disposal, attacks crime. Moreover, *authoritative aggression* occurs whenever the authority conferred by position is used to set upon or attack subordinates.

Altruistic power is the ability to generate, through another's love or altruism, positive interests in the direction of one's own. *Altruistic aggression* is the attacking of others on the basis of this love. The love for a leader, for mankind, for God, has been the basis of attacks on others. The love of a Christian God in part led to the Crusades, and today we have the altruistic —mankind-loving—aggression bound in such ideas as "ending capitalist exploitation," "ending tyranny," "creating social justice," and "overthrowing the system." Guerrilla attacks, terrorism, political assassinations, and religious wars have their basis in the induction of some political formula, some solution to man's ills. Today's ideological wars are altruistic combat among visions of the good life. And the inductive power of a political leader lies in his ability to connect the love of man for his species, God, or country, to the formula he provides.

Altruistic aggression is not limited to collective action. Through the love of his mistress, a man may induce her to kill his wife; through the love of her child, a mother may heed his cries for help and attack his assailant; and through the love of his country, a man may be induced to assassinate a president.

Finally, there is the aggressive style of manipulative power, the control over potentialities or opportunities. *Manipulative aggression* is then such offensive control. For example, propaganda may lead a person to hate, to attack members of another group, class, or race. Indoctrination may cause a person to assail an evil economic-political system. Desire for control over a situation may provoke a person to attack another, as when a sergeant deliberately goads a private until, tired, frustrated, and angry, he strikes out at his tormentor, thus providing a legal basis for a court martial. The enlisted man aggressed, but it was a manipulated aggression.

In sum, aggression is a style, an offensive manifesting or manifestation of power. It is inseparably linked to and takes on the form of power. Thus we can speak of identive, assertive, or forceful nonsocial aggression; or of coercive, bargaining, intellectual, authoritative, inductive, or manipulative social aggression. These pure forms, of course, are rarely manifested singly. Most situations reflect a combination of aggressive forms, with perhaps one dominating. Thus the military attack of one nation on another can manifest coercive aggression (an attempt to change the will of the nation opposing the demands of the first), forceful aggression (an attempt to bypass the other's will and to eradicate his capability to resist),[18] manipulative aggression (in whipping up hostile sentiment), and altruistic aggression (in inducing men to fight in the belief that man's welfare would be improved if the battle were won). Revolutions are similarly such a mixture.

Aggression seen in this light shows the simplicity of arguments that it is environmental, instinctual, or due to frustration. Multidimensional and multifold, tied to the various forms of power, aggression is a complex of different forms melded in a single act. Let us see how aggression so understood contrasts with some conventional views.

Does aggression involve hostile injury or harm to another? Hostile injury or harm is neither a sufficient nor a necessary condition for aggression in my terms. In defense against a mugger, for example, one may inflict hostile injury. Moreover, injury or harm may or may not be involved even in forceful[19] or coercive[20] aggression, as well as the other forms of power. In other words, injury and violence may occur, but there is no synonymy between such occurrences and aggression. The focus in the literature on aggression as harm or injury (without considering whether it is defensive) is a focus on secondary and partial phenomena, like a study of the nature of an elephant that concentrates on the waves it makes in a pond.

Does aggressiveness comprise hostility or anger toward another? Not necessarily. As a style of manifesting power, no particular emotion may be involved. Aggression may be instrumental. Again, it may be the one acting defensively, protecting himself or his values, who is hostile or angry. To be sure, assertive aggression can involve attacks on others manifesting paranoidal hostility. But this is not to say that aggression always comprises hostility.

Is certain behavior aggression, such as physically attacking another, invading another's territory, or assaulting another with a club? Not necessarily. What is offensive as apart from defensive or neutral behavior is culturally and situationally defined. Placing a man on a table and cutting him open with a knife may be surgery, religious sacrifice, a warrior rite, or torture. Striking another with a club may be a sport, an attack, or a defense. In some cultures merely crossing another man's shadow is interpreted as an act of aggression on that person's spirit. The ultimate aggression is presumed to be killing another, yet such activities as carrying the old to a secluded spot to die, infanticide, and euthanasia have been culturally sanctioned as neutral behavior. Even within the same culture, there are different views of what constitutes killing. Witness the debate over abortion, a practice that some feel is an act of aggression against a living fetus. To focus on an objective behavior to define aggression is to commit the typical behavioral physicalistic fallacy. It is not what is physical that counts to man, but rather the perspective through which he manifests reality, the meanings and values this reality has for him.

Is aggression, then, an intention to do harm? Aggression can be intentional, but some acts occur unconsciously as in the identive aggression of a crying, kicking infant. Moreover, the intent to do harm can exist without the quality of being offensive, as in a police unit defending itself against a guerrilla attack.

In short, aggression as the offensive manifesting of power can be, but is not necessarily, instrumental nor intentional, and it may involve anger and hostility, injury and destructiveness, or certain acts or actions, although these might not be present. It is this subjective, multidimensional, multiform nature of manifest aggression that scientists and scholars have seen and defined differently. The latent definition underlying this variety, the core meaning in aggression, is as a vector of power toward offensive manifestation.

2.3 TEMPERAMENT AND NEEDS

The relationship of aggression to man psychologically depends on its associated form of power. Identive aggression is an offensive manifesting of being, an unconscious thrusting outward toward reality of man's physical or psychological dispositions, of his individuality. Physically, this may be his size, manner of movement, and appearance; psychologically, his temperament and unconscious needs.

Temperament involves a person's characteristic behavior. It is patterned behavior, a consistent syndrome that does not vary dependent on gratification or satisfaction, as does behavior resulting from needs or drives. Temperament is also multidimensional in that the character of a person forms a psychological profile across a number of common temperamental components found among all men. For example,[21] one such temperamental component is affectothymia versus sizothymia, or the tendency to be outgoing, good-natured, easygoing, cooperative, soft-hearted, attentive to people, and trustful versus being reserved, critical, grasping, obstructive, cool, aloof, hard, and suspicious.

Another is ego strength (stability) versus emotionality and neuroticism, or the tendency to be steady, calm, realistic about problems, mature, and lacking neurotic fatigue versus changeability, emotional impulsiveness, avoidance of necessary decisions, the inability to tolerate frustration, and neurotic fatigue. A third temperamental component is surgency versus desurgency, or the propensity to be happy-go-lucky, cheerful, sociable, energetic, humorous, talkative, and placid versus a

TABLE 2.1
THE TEMPERAMENTAL COMPONENT OF
DOMINANCE VERSUS SUBMISSIVENESS[a]

Dominance	versus	Submissiveness
Self-assertive, confident	vs.	Submissive, unsure
Boastful, conceited	vs.	Modest, retiring
Aggressive,[b] pugnacious	vs.	Complacent
Extra-punitive	vs.	Impunitive, intropunitive
Vigorous, forceful	vs.	Meek, quiet
Willful, egotistic	vs.	Obedient

a. From Cattell (1965:90).
b. Cattell does not define aggression, but the context implies that it is a tendency to fight or attack others, to be quarrelsome.

sober character, depressed, seclusive, subdued, dull, taciturn, and unable to relax. Character is a consistent behavior made up of such components.

Now, as a matter of character, some people consistently and generally manifest more identive aggression than others. Is there then a particular temperamental component of character associated with such aggression? Yes, *the dominance versus submissiveness component,*[22] which manifests the behavior associated with aggression in both primates and humans. Table 2.1 lists the manifestations of this temperament.

The dominating temperament is strongly self-assertive, confident, and adventurous, but also tends to anger, quarrelsomeness, and destructiveness.

As would be expected from our experience with aggression among primates, dominance as a form of aggression is most manifest in males. Among females dominance becomes a composed (versus shy or bashful), poised, hypochondriac, and to a lesser extent, reserved, secretive, and independent minded temperament. In young children a dominating temperament goes along with disobedience, teasing, insensitiveness, not respecting the property of others, bossing, and attacking verbally and physically.

In other animals, the dominance pattern has been found associated with masculine sexual aggression, grabbing food from others, and bullying, as well as concentration of the male hormone (testosterone).

In apes, this temperament includes initiating most fighting, never cringing under aggression, mounting subordinates regardless of sex, pre-empting food supply, being more active, initiating more play, and doing more grooming.

In mental outpatients, the dominance temperament involves a lack of guilt feeling, little need of approval, strong assertiveness, and overt expression of hostility. Among psychotics, it includes bullying and aggressiveness, being assaultive, obscene, irritable, critical and sarcastic, having temper outbursts; and the use of projection to escape unacceptable drives. [Rummel, 1975:218]

Clearly, dominance is a temperament manifesting what most have associated with aggression in the literature.[23] And it is of mixed genetic and environmental origin (Cattell, 1957:111). Heredity seems to contribute most to its variation from one family to another, whereas differences within families seem to be due mainly to environment.

The dominance temperament is a major contributor to character-rooted identive aggression. A second temperament, which also contributes to such aggression, is a paranoidal (suspicious) versus an inner-relaxed (trusting) component. This manifests the paranoidal hostility that Storr (1968) associates with man's aggression. The paranoidal (Cattell, 1957:143-146) person is suspicious, jealous, self-sufficient, and withdrawn, whereas the inner-relaxed person is trusting, understanding, composed, and socially at home. Those who are paranoidal

are also aggressive, short tempered, extra-punitive, hostile, and feel systematically persecuted. Paranoidal psychotics, especially, are assaultive, uncooperative, delusioned, and obsessed, and mental outpatients have been found with obsessively hostile impulses, and high tension.

This temperament appears both in normal and abnormal people (who tend to be at the extremes of temperament) and is distinct from paranoid schizophrenia (which has been found as a separate temperament also existing in normal people). Those with a tendency toward the paranoidal end are basically characterized by high tension handled by projection as a defense mechanism, and by suspicion and hostility. Therefore, that aggression should also be part of or a result of temperament is understandable. [Rummel, 1975:218-219]

In sum, then, we find that aggression as an unconscious, offensive behavior against reality is partially a pattern of behavior that varies among men along dominance versus submissiveness and paranoidal versus inner-relaxed temperaments. Identive aggression is therefore characteristic of some but not all men. It is in part hereditary, in part environmental, in part a matter of temperament.

But man not only is temperamentally inclined, he is also motivated to behave in certain ways. He has urges, drives, or needs. To what degree does man's motivational structure contribute to identive aggression? First, I must clarify the difference between needs and drives.

By *need* I mean an *innate* psycho-physical potential, which when actualized is a cluster of dispositions associated with specific emotions (such as feeling hungry), a common goal (food), provocative situations (the smell of bacon and eggs cooking), and goal gratification (eating). The need itself depends on the constitutional nature of a person in addition to the history of how the need has been satisfied.

Moreover, the strength of the actualized need depends on a person's physiological state in relation to the degree of associated goal gratification.

A *drive* is that part of an actualized need referring to the purely physiological urge in relation to the physiological gratification received. It is inherent in the person and is that which is felt irrespective of external stimulation. Need is therefore the broader concept, not only involving the drive, but also the constitutional and hereditary nature of the individual (for example, some have constitutionally stronger sex drives than others), his past history of gratification, and the overall present satisfactions of the need. [Rummel, 1975:198]

A need therefore constitutes psychophysical dispositions toward particular goals, actions, and emotions. It is a complex of attitudes. A drive, a part of a need, is the state of a purely innate physiological urge in relation to its gratification. For example, everyone has a sex drive. As expressed in needs, however, the drive is differentiated. Differing sexual potency, and varying cultural and environmental influences, affect the inner expression of this drive and associated emotion. Some gratify this drive through a *need* for homosexual relations; others *need* certain perversions.

With this understanding, I use the broader and more attitude-linked concept of need and ask: Does man have any aggressive needs? Multivariate research, through a variety of empirical analyses, has determined the existence of seven core needs relating to sex, hunger, gregariousness, protectiveness, curiosity, security, and self-assertion.[24] In addition, evidence is accumulating for a need to express pugnacity.[25] Pugnacity is akin to sadism. It is a need to fight, hurt, attack, damage, destroy, or get revenge. It involves hostility and the associated emotion of rage or anger. Clearly, this description is of an aggressive need-drive, as often defined in the literature. And so it is recognized by the multivariate researchers who have uncovered it. Cattell and Warburton (1967:176) label it a "pugnacity of aggression erg [sic]." In Cattell and Horn (1959:22), it is "pugnacity-sadism" (for Fromm, a component of malignant aggression) of which is said "The popular term 'aggressiveness' seems to cover this and assertiveness."[26]

Is this need an aggressive urge in my terms, that is, an urge to the offensive manifestation of power? Yes. Once activated, a need pressures man to seek its gratification. He may absorb this pressure into the pursuit of his superordinate goal, or block it internally if in conflict with this goal. Nonetheless, the need is appetitive, driving man to seek its gratification. Surely, then, to gratify pugnacity (such as in revenge), man will resort to offensive behavior, to the pushing, thrusting, besetting manner so characteristic of aggression, to initiating and provoking violence.

However aggression comprises not only violence, but also a thrusting of the self, a will-to-power of being. Is a need associated with this kind of offensive assertion? Yes, the need for self-assertion and its associated emotion of pride. This is a status-striving need, a driving to exceed one's fellows and rise in the pecking order.[27] Self-assertion is a need to establish one's self, a striving to reach one's level. Surely this is an aspect of aggression as I have defined it. Self-assertion implies an initiating action, a moving into another's territory, a pushing against the status quo.

Besides pugnacity and self-assertion, there are the security and protectiveness needs. Insecurity (or the need to escape),[28] and its emotion of fear, form a source of defensive aggression, the benign aggression described by Fromm (1973). When fundamental being or values are threatened, when risking death, financial loss, or military invasion, one may lash out. A cornered man often attacks, such action is no less aggression for being provoked by fear and threat.

The protectiveness (parental or succorance) need is, I believe, basic to understanding contemporary collective violence. It involves care of the young, especially one's children, but also extends to concern for the welfare of man and acts of altruism. It is the need underlying the desire to improve man's lot, as well as the aggressive instrumentalities associated with this, and its associated emotion is pity (compassion, humanity, charity, sympathy, empathy). Parents will aggressively defend (and advance) their offspring, people will sometimes aggressively jump to the aid of those in distress (as bystanders leap in to restrain a man from beating his wife), and man collectively will attack the "evils" of capitalism, communism, fascism, racism, sexism.

One final need is less solidly based in the scientific evidence than self-assertion, but there is systematic support for its existence. Psychotherapists have long recognized narcissism (Cattell, 1972:246; Cattell and Horn, 1959:22; Cattell and Warburton, 1967:185), which Fromm (1973:200-205) treated as an important source of aggression. Narcissism is a need to gratify the self sensually, to self-love, to have an easy life. It is self-indulgence. Its accompanying emotion is sensuousness.

Such are man's common needs, which together with his character-rooted sources of aggression, explain the unconscious tendency of man to offensively manifest his power. In summary, the unconscious sources of aggression are multi-dimensional. On the one hand aggression is seated in man's common and independent needs of pugnacity, self-assertion, security, protectiveness, and narcissism. Fed by man's associated emotions and feelings of anger and rage, pride, fear, pity, and sensuality, it waxes and wanes, depending on the stimulation of these needs and their gratification. On the other hand, aggression is partly rooted in character. It is also temperament, an individual's style or manner of behaving, which involves both dominating others and a tendency toward paranoia. Thus Freud, Lorenz, and Storr are correct to a degree. Fromm is also correct. And the environmentalists and learning theorists? They also have a point, as the next section reveals. We have here the perception of the same reality from different perspectives, a reality comprising the dynamic psychological field.

2.4 ATTITUDES AND INTERESTS

As described in *The Conflict Helix* (Section 6.3), attitudes are want-goal-means dispositions connecting to man's needs. They are absorbed from our culture, forged in our family and interpersonal relations, and developed through experience. Needs become energized, associated attitudes become activated, and behavioral dispositions are manifest. Activated attitudes are interests—powers toward the realization of specific goals in order to satisfy particular wants.

It is within the dynamic calculus of attitudes that man's sentiments and roles lie. Whereas the needs define man's id, the attitudes are organized into an integrated self, reality oriented (ego) and morally conscious (superego), that direct action toward the superordinate goal of self-esteem. The ego is formed through transactions with social reality, and the superego embodies cultural values and morality.

It is within this dynamic system of attitudes that cultural learning and experience play their roles. Mankind shares the same needs, but not the same culture or experience. Environment shapes the attitudes that will gratify needs. The same protective need may be gratified through fifteen years of close supervision and training of the child in one culture, and casting him off at age ten in another; it may be satisfied through forced missionary conversion of heathens, or through respect for different beliefs. The same security need can be stimulated by fear of a shaman, a god, inflation, or nuclear war.

Events, objects, and situations take on subjective meaning depending on the cultural matrix through which we interpret reality, and on our personal history. A pugnacity need may be gratified by sticking pins in an enemy's effigy, making a culturally indecent gesture toward him, purposely stepping on his shadow, spreading malicious gossip about him, or belting him one. Thus it is incorrect to characterize a need by certain specific acts. A need is reflected in certain emotions, such as fear, pity, and pride. How these emotions and underlying needs work themselves out in behavior depends on the attitudinal interface developed through culture and experience. Certain types of attitudes, nonetheless, connect to specific needs, otherwise these needs could never be identified. For example, pugnacity connects to attitudes involving attacking and fighting others. The precise behavior, however, whether stomping on someone's flower garden or kicking the person in the shins, is a matter of individual learning. As any academic soon learns, there are many ways of attacking and cutting up a rival without lifting a finger in anger.

Here we have the heavy hand of culture and the precise mechanisms of social learning. Through both, man may develop aggressive (offensive) attitudes—aggressive goals and means— which gratify his needs and are a danger to himself and others. On the other hand, he may learn to gratify his needs in part through "benign" aggressive attitudes and the replacement of aggressive means-goals linkages with solidary, conciliatory, consensual attitudes.[29]

Most important, such attitudes are organized into a reality-testing, moral self striving for self-esteem. Much depends on what the esteem is based on. If, for a gang member, it is his ability to beat up an old lady, his esteem will be linked to such aggressive attitudes, and this aggression will be an integrated part of his behavior. A soldier in combat whose self-esteem is linked to his buddies' opinion of him, may be an aggressive killer of the enemy in striving for approval. If esteem is tied to command and coercive power over others, one may ape the more successful and aggressive villains in movies and television.

The keys to understanding environmentally based aggression are man's dynamic attitudes as they are integrated into a self striving for esteem. Intentional aggression occurs at the level of attitudes. Whether aggression is assertive, coercive, bargaining, authoritative, inductive, and so on, is a matter of the intentions, of the goals and means, of the self.

Indentive aggression is unconscious, a manifesting of being. Intentional aggression is goal directed, involving acts and actions, reason and morality. What then is the connection between temperament, needs, and attitudes? Temperament is the style of our reflex behavior, of our practices (custom, etiquette), and of achieving our goals. Our goal, for example, may not be to dominate another, but we may do do simply by character. Thus temperament, which is partly hereditary, partly influenced by environment, helps fashion the manifesting of our interests. Needs, however, energize attitudes and drive man to gratify them. Pugnacity, self-assertion, security, protectiveness, and narcissism may provide inherent aggressive urges, but the attitudinal means-goals and their scope and intensity linking these needs to acts or action is a matter of learning and culture. And these attitudes are under the control of a self and will striving for self-esteem.

2.5 PERCEPTION, EXPECTATIONS, AND BEHAVIORAL DISPOSITIONS

Needs are stimulated within a perceived situation in which man has certain behavioral dispositions and expectations about the outcome of his behavior. To emphasize temperament, needs, or attitudes in discussing aggression is to forget that character and motivations are contextually keyed, and that associated behavior is situationally selected from a repertoire.

Consider the situation first. Man's perception is a dialectical outcome of a confrontation between reality's powers bearing on him and his outward directed perspective. An aspect of this perspective consists of the cultural schema and meanings-values-norms through which stimuli are interpreted. There can be no perception without interpretation. And through this interpretation man contributes to manifesting the dispositions of reality.

We are not born with a way of perceiving reality other than with our physiological equipment. Since perception is a meaning-endowing process, it is gradually learned through man's culture and by trial and error. Moreover, the process does not end with interpretation through the cultural matrix. What is interpreted automatically, unconsciously, becomes a conscious percept only within the total psychological field. Field forces may alter perceptions to maintain cognitive balance, to conform with a person's hopes, wishes, or preconceptions, or to contribute to defensive delusion or projections. We often see what we want to see.

Clearly, perception is crucial to understanding aggression. For offensive behavior is directed toward a situation, and the direction and nature of that behavior depend on our perception of that situation. Needs are partly energized from within (a growing hunger, an increasing sexual desire), partly stimulated from without (the smell of bacon cooking, seeing an erotic movie). But stimulation requires perception, and this becomes a matter of interpretation and the forces bearing on perception within the field. One man's pugnacity may be aroused by a perceived slur on his race, another by the perceived surliness of a clerk, a third by the perceived inconsiderateness of another driver. We interpret and thereby transform our world. And the world we create may be peopled by insults, threats, aggressiveness to which we respond with fear, pity, anger. But the world is partly of ourselves, of our culture and experience melded through the psychological field into our reality-transforming perspective.

The case is similar with attitudes, which link needs to concrete means-ends behavior. Attitudes are energized into interests by needs, but their keying to reality depends on our perception of that reality; their content is situational. Consider the concept "police" as a part of an attitude. This cultural construct consisting of certain percepts (nature and color of clothing, weapon, size) embodies expectations of certain behaviors and a sense of legitimacy (or exploitation, depending on the subculture). The concept of "police" within an attitude is a meaning-value-norm complex, and the linkage of the associated attitude with a given situation is a perceptual keying in of this complex. Thus the situation of a white policeman frisking a black person on the street can be perceived as "arrest" or as "black subjugation."

Normally nonaggressive people become quite aggressive if they perceive threats to their security, attacks on their values, or slurs on their self. But they must learn what constitutes a threat, an attack, or a slur. What interest will thereby become engaged, whether to attack, to defend, to flee, to ignore, is a matter of the perceptual linkage of these interests to the situation.

With temperament, too, the case is similar. Man's character is manifested in behavior that is situationally directed and linked. Whether it is a matter of aggressively dominating others or reacting with paranoidal hostility, the object of such behavior must be perceived. Again, a particular interpretation of reality will influence the direction of such behavior. By character, we may aggress against those above us in a hierarchy but cooperate with those below us who, we perceive, accept our status. By character, we may be hostile to those perceived to be "out to get us." And by character, we may bully those who, in our perception, are weak and ineffectual.

Perception is the interface between man and external reality. It is the matrix through which man's innate and character-rooted aggressiveness is transformed.

Whatever the perceived situation, however, man's behavior is not fixed, not preprogrammed within his genes. Man has a repertoire of behaviors, a multifold, multidimensional variety of actions defining his culture and delineating his society. These accumulate from experience, from learning and individual experimentation, from trial and error, and from the example of others, forming his space of potential behaviors and behavioral dispositions, a space physiologically bounded, of course, but dimensioned by our culture and experience.

What is considered to be aggressive behavior in one culture may not be potential forms of behavior within another. Revolution or riot may be inconceivable and unknown; war, unthinkable and unrealized; political murder, unimaginable and absurd. It is true that many modern forms of collective aggression are passed from culture to culture, like useful technological innovations.

Within any situation[30] man is disposed to behave in a certain way, depending on his needs, interests, temperament, and moods and states. The nature of these dispositions depends on the behaviors available to him in his behavior space. How he does behave, however, is a matter of the expectations that weight his choice. Like behaviors, expectations are wholly learned. They are norms, customs, implicit rules of behavior, social roles[31] that are forged through experience and trial and error. Through social learning a person comes to expect reward or punishment from certain behaviors, and these expectations weigh on his behavioral dispositions.[32] Although disposed to behave aggressively, a person may act differently because he fears expected criticism, ostracism, or a public scene. On the other hand, although not disposed to behave aggressively, a person may select such behavior because of the respect and prestige (as with a gang member) he believes would thereby incur. In either case, a person may behave aggressively or nonaggressively as we anticipate such behavior from others.

2.6 MOODS AND STATES

Often unmentioned in the literature is the influence on aggressive behavior of man's mood or state. If ill, fatigued, hot, or very hungry, he can be irritable and touchy; he may lash out and attack. Some have claimed that urban riots take place mainly during the hot summer months for these reasons. No doubt there are more basic causes, but it is also likely that man's physiological state influences his aggressiveness.

2.7 THE PSYCHOLOGICAL FIELD OF AGGRESSION

I have briefly considered the structures of the psychological field in their relation to aggression. My purpose is not a complete elucidation, but a clarification within a direction. I wish to show that aggression is multidimensional, that its psychological foundations are complex, and that the connections between the sources of aggression within man and his observable behavior are multifold. That instincts produce aggression, that drives generate aggression, that learning creates aggression—each proposition, standing by itself, is a simplistic theory. All dimensions are present to some degree and are simultaneously part of a field of relationships and dynamic forces that can modify, dampen, or inflate aggressive impulses, attitudes, and behavioral dispositions. The whole is a complex of perception, personality, behavioral dispositions, and expectations. To emphasize one without the others within the field is to forget that man is always a feeling-thinking-doing, integrated totality.

This means that pugnacity or self-assertion or protectiveness may be aroused, but no aggression may occur because the self wills otherwise, because no triggering situation is perceived, because expectations suggest defensive behavior, or because one's mood is inappropriate. On the other hand, a person may act aggressively even though such needs are satiated, because it is in his character to do so in the perceived situation. Finally, needs or character aside, a person may act aggressively in the pursuit of his superordinate goal. Aggression may be a learned instrumentality for achieving self-esteem, for striving upward. To understand aggression as the offensive manifesting of interests, therefore, is to understand man as personality-situation-dispositions-expectations, as needs-attitudes-interests-temperament, as id-ego-superego, as field-self-will.

2.8 AND THE CONFLICT HELIX

How does aggression so understood relate to the conflict helix—the process of social conflict? First, in restricting the discussion to aggression within this process, I am focusing on intentional aggression. Manifest social conflict involves willful actions guided by the self to achieve specific interests through another. Second, we must keep in mind that aggression is subjective. It is contextual. The same objective act can be aggressive or defensive depending on its meaning and the actor's intent within a situation.

The conflict helix moves through potentiality, conflict-structure, conflict-situation, initiation, balancing, balance and the structure of expectations, disruption, and a new twist of the conflict cycle. Aggression may be present during all these phases. It may be potentiality lying within man's meanings, values, norms, and statuses. It may be dispositional as part of man's dynamic calculus—his system of attitudes contributing to the structure of conflict—and his behavioral dispositions. It may be an aspect of opposing interests and associated expectations. It may be the manner in which the will tries to manifest its interests and woven through the balancing phase. Capability to aggress and its credibility may underlie the resulting balancing, the disruption of the structure of expectations may be manifest through aggression.

Aggressive energy from activated needs can add power to the conflict process, and the scope, direction, and intensity of that process can be influenced by learned aggressive attitudes and temperaments. Moreover, since conflict is opposition, and *the manifestation of opposition requires initiation,* social aggression as offensively manifesting social interests is woven into the very nature of the process. That is, *aggression does not cause conflict.* Rather, aggression innately characterizes the manifesting process. Aggressive needs add fuel to the process; aggressive attitudes add substance; aggressive temperaments add style.

But the social process itself is seated in man's social relationships. Conflict is an adjustment to changing circumstances, and aggression is a characteristic of that process. Where there is environmental stability and interpersonal relations have become locked together in overlapping, crosscutting, and intersecting expectations, nested upward into a crystallized cultural system, there is little social aggression. Thus so-called aggressive primates live together in harmony under stable conditions; human tribes manifest little social aggression if they have lived for generations in a stable environment; modern man shows little social aggression in a stable network of norms and expectations. Let there be disruption, or rapid change, upsetting expectations and norms, and the conflict helix takes another twist, with social aggression becoming manifest.

The mistake of the instinctualist, the drive theorists, and the behaviorist, of ethology (à la Lorenz), psychotherapy, and social learning theory, is not in wrongly identifying a source of aggression. All are partly correct. Aggression *is* partly instinctual, partly drive, partly character, partly learned. But their analyses have been static, physicalistic, and asocial—a physical study of crossed sticks without an analysis of the subjective meaning of cross in human interaction.[33] Regardless of source, aggression is a wholly subjective manifestation within a conflict *process.*

NOTES

1. For the treatment of instinct as a psychological issue, see Birney and Teevan (1961). For a classic attack on the belief that man has instincts, see Bernard (1924), and for a current counterview, see Fletcher (1957). For an ethological treatment of instinct, see Tinbergen (1951).

2. Lorenz put ethology on the social scientist's map. For a well-written popularization of Lorenz's view on man's "instinctual aggressive drive," see Ardrey (1966, 1970).

3. See, for example, the collection of reviews and articles in Ashley Montagu (1973).

4. See the many negative reviews in Montagu (1973). Johnson (1972) and Fromm (1973) summarize some of the contra-Lorenz findings on animals. See also Carthy and Ebling (1964).

5. "... we have already argued that territoriality cannot be conceived as a species property, like leg length or plumage pattern; rather it is a group characteristic expressing the effects of the interaction of individuals with one another and the environment. Territory is but a single aspect of the social system shown by a species. An understanding of the system as a whole is more likely to inform us regarding territory than will the particular study of territory to the neglect of other social behaviours" (Crook, 1973:203).

6. "Every animal species lives within a social structure characteristic for this species. Whether hierarchical or not, it is the frame of reference to which the animal's behavior is adapted. A tolerable social equilibrium is a necessary condition for its existence. Its destruction through crowding constitutes a massive threat to the animal's existence, and intense aggression is the result one would expect, given the defensive role of aggression, especially when flight is impossible" (Fromm, 1973:106).

7. I am relying here on the selections from Adler's early writings presented by Ansbacher and Ansbacher (1956:34-39).

8. My own perspective on man has been influenced by Adler, especially my emphasis on understanding man teleologically through his superordinate goal.

9. See also Hannah Arendt (1969), who makes this one of her major observations.

10. For a clear and brief summary of Freud's views on aggression, see Storr (1968). A more extended and complete analysis is given by Fromm (1973) in an appendix.

11. Fromm's observations on self-assertion, on the importance of meaning (e.g., it is the meaning that frustration has that is important in producing aggression [p. 678]), on the integrating and directing function of central goals, and on the role of impotence, overlap in perspective with those of Adler and May. Indeed, in many ways Fromm's view on aggression appears as a compromise between the psycho-analytic outlook and the Adler-May standpoint.

Significantly, Fromm nowhere in his book mentions Adler, who formulated the first psychological theory of aggression while a member of Freud's Vienna psychoanalytic circle and is alleged to have said later in life, "I enriched psychoanalysis by the aggressive drive. I gladly make them a present of it" (Bottome, 1939:64).

12. Italics omitted.

13. Fromm seems to adopt a Marxist interpretation of society and to lean heavily toward socialism. On the other hand, he emphasizes freedom (above equality) and favors a decentralization of authority (p. 216); in this Fromm seems to be more an anarcholibertarian, but his would be hardly consistent with socialism in practice.

14. The index to Ford and Urban's *Systems of Psychotherapy* (1963) gives only six references to aggression: three to a discussion of Freud's work, one to Adler's, and two to Karen Horney's. Horney (1945) was a Freudian who broke with orthodox psychoanalysis to stress the role of learning in creating disordered behavior, and the importance of patterns of behavior developed within the family.

15. In emphasizing a social definition of aggression, as does Bandura (1973:8), for example, social learning theory has made a significant advance over other theories. Rarely is it recognized that what constitutes an attack, an injury, or forceful behavior is a cultural matter. Most theories assume aggression to have objective characteristics, yet one culture's aggression may be another's healing practice, religious ritual, or athletic event.

16. The first behavioral statement of this theory was by J. Dollard et al., in their well-known *Frustration and Aggression* (1939), in which they asserted that aggression always results from frustration (p. 1). This extreme position has been qualified by subsequent researchers to incorporate the influence of learning, perception, and expectations. Frustration is now seen as a predisposing rather than triggering cause (Megargee, 1972:9-11).

17. This is a favored observation used to counter the theory that aggression is instinctual. See, for example, Fromm (1973) and the reviews of Lorenz in Montagu (1973), where this point is often made. Those using this argument often neglect to consider that aggression is subjective in meaning. A stare in one culture may be as aggressive as a slap in another. To anticipate my discussion below, it is the self-assertive and forceful meaning of aggression that is important in intercultural comparisons, not an objective manifestation such as physical violence.

Second, those using the comparative culture argument deal with structures, not dynamics. Surely, cross-sectionally, some cultures manifest little aggression. They may live in harmonious equilibrium, established over centuries, with their environment and with their neighbors. But let the environment be modified—by the exhaustion of land to be divided among villagers, by the introduction of new tools, or by natural disasters—and the rapidly changing situation will create aggression of a more physical variety, simply because physical aggression is instrumental for establishing new fundamental relationships in a situation of change and uncertainty.

18. The distinction here is between war fought over a particular policy, or war fought to defeat the other party to the point of unconditional surrender. The first is coercive, since the attempt is to influence the other's will; the second is forceful, since the attempt is to destroy the other's ability to do as it wills. World War II saw the application of forceful power by the United States; in the Vietnam War there was application of coercion.

19. For example, police may forcefully restrain a suspect and carry him to the police station without hurting him. Yet, this is forceful aggression.

20. For example, kidnappers may abduct and threaten to kill a child if his millionaire parents refuse to pay a ransom. This is aggressive coercion, but if the ransom is paid, the child may be returned unharmed.

21. The following examples are from Cattell (1965, Chapters 3-4).

22. The major scientific evidence for this temperament is given in Cattell (1957:108-110). See also Cattell (1965:89-91).

23. The dominance temperament manifests that behavior Lorenz most associates with aggression. Moreover, the character-rooted malignant aggression Fromm describes would reflect, in my terms, a dominating temperament. Fromm is one of the few to uncouple a type of aggression from needs, drives, or instinct, and seat it in character, as I have done here.

24. Rummel, 1975, pages 199-200.

25. Pugnacity is included as a need by Horn (1966:633) and by Cattell (1965:190, 315). Cattell and his colleagues include tests for pugnacity in their personality-motivation questionnaires (Cattell and Horn, 1959; Cattell and Warburton, 1967).

26. I discuss assertiveness later.

27. This is a need that has been consistently uncovered in multivariate motivational research. See Horn (1966), Cattell (1957), and Cattell and Warburton (1967). The scientific-quantitative findings on these needs and the aforementioned temperaments are scattered through hundreds of research articles and books. Therefore, I have focused on the leader and major synthesizer of this research, the one whose works generally reference the other literature. I am not basing my discussion on the personal speculations or experience of one man or school of psychological thought, but on more than twenty years of systematic, programmatic scientific research into man's dynamic motivational structure.

28. In one place, Cattell and Horn (1959:22) call this an escape erg.

29. I do not mean to imply that this is desirable in some larger ethical sense. To seek justice and the Good may require some aggressive attitudes. Cultures may stagnate and man may be impotent without some channels for aggressive individuality. However, these are questions aside from my interest here, which is to determine the nature of aggression from the psychological field perspective.

30. Henceforth, "situation," unqualified stands for a subjective, perceived situation.

31. Roles are two sided, consisting from one perspective as a pattern of role expectations, from another as a cluster of attitudes sharing the same means.

32. Expectations do not determine behavior, but they weight behavioral dispositions. We are less inclined to behave in a way that will elicit punishment. However we may so behave, even if the punishment is severe. If a dictator demands upon threat of jail that we lie to help convict and execute a friend, we may choose jail. Man is guided by his perceptions of right and wrong, as well as by reward and punishment. Through man's bloody history, many have willingly chosen death, the ultimate punishment, instead of doing evil.

33. Adler is an exception to this, as is Rollo May. Both, however, have focused on the individual, not the interpersonal process.

Chapter 3

FRUSTRATION, DEPRIVATION,
AND AGGRESSION

The popularity of reformist liberalism in the academic community gives the deprivation and access doctrines appeal and persuasiveness. But it also leads those threatened by social change to reject the social sciences, the professors, and the bureaucrats, undermining their effectiveness as objective brokers of social change. Many academics cannot understand why steps taken in accord with such theories frequently intensify the demands of the insurgents and escalate both frontlash and backlash; they cannot understand their being rejected by the new militant leaders, who consider reformist ideologies a variety of tokenism. They fail to grasp the dimensions of political bargaining reflected by cries of revolution and black power, which can be understood only in terms of bargaining equations underlying legalistic abstractions and economic improvements. It is the bargaining equations that determine whether progress toward reform will dampen extremism or encourage it.

Nieburg, 1969:43

3.1 FRUSTRATION

Man strives to gratify his wants and desires, his goals, aims, and ambitions. Introspection and self-knowledge make this much self-evident; experience with others confirms the generalization.

Moreover, man is often unable to satisfy his desires or accomplish his goals. Sometimes his ambitions exceed his abilities, or he misperceives the possibilities. But sometimes he is blocked by an external barrier that precludes gratification.

This may be a traffic jam preventing him from reaching an appointment, a college rule prohibiting him from taking a particular course, an amorous neighborhood tom cat interrupting sleep, or his race restricting professional advancement. Whatever the barrier, a person is frustrated. We all are frustrated from time to time.

In addition, we all have experienced irritation and anger at some frustrations. A long line preventing us from seeing an eagerly awaited movie, a crush of shoppers hindering the purchase of some simple necessities, a slow driver obstructing a narrow road, probably have aroused in all of us that familiar flush of annoyance, even anger. That frustration of our desires and goals occasionally leads to anger is a commonplace. It is subjectively unquestionable—a fact of our existence.

Of course, not all frustrations lead to anger. Indeed, it is more common to accept frustration—the blockage of our wants or goals—as feedback suggesting that we adjust or alter our aims. We do this automatically, hour by hour, day by day. Frustration signals the error in the trial-and-error process by which we dialectically adjust our perspectives to external powers and potentialities. To live, to assert oneself, is to be hindered, to face difficulties, *to be opposed.* My desire to write this section uninterruptedly is hindered by construction noise in the background; my desire for physical comfort is defeated by the summer heat; my search for the right words to express my "understanding" is blocked by the barrier between structured language and unstructured "insight" and feelings. Moreover, when I let my consciousness stroll through the nested levels of my existence, I am also aware of a multitude of frustrations that reach consciousness like a flock of pheasants startled out of tall grass. Frustrations associated with family, research, teaching, politics, and the growing structure of coercive rules and laws. As I write, my life is within a matrix of such frustrations, high and low, large and small, significant and trivial.

Yet at the moment I am content, relatively happy, and feel no irritation, no anger.

Besides man's desires and goals, his frustrations and anger, there are two other commonplace facts of life. Man sometimes desires or aims to injure or hurt others, and behaves in such a manner, sometimes because of his frustrations. Again, in our subjective world, these two facts are incontestable. Our awareness of them enables us to better perceive others,[1] to adjust our interests and interactions, and to develop predictive expectations. We can then understand why on a hot day in slow city traffic, one motorist will attack another for blocking his path, why a parent whose losing bridge game is interrupted for the fifth time by a child will vigorously spank him, and why a mistress cast off by her lover will send poison pen letters to his wife.

In the late 1930s, the commonplace enabling us to understand such behavior in certain contexts was erected into an invariant law of nature by a group of Yale psychologists (Dollard et al., 1939). First, they equated aggression with the desire to hurt or injure others. This effectively confused the various forms of aggression with one overt manifestation and confounded the bases of aiming to harm another, which may be instrumental (as in spanking a child), defensive (as in kicking an attacker), or hostile (as in spreading malicious gossip). Were one to equate love with kissing, the conceptual, cognitive confusion would be no less.

Second, frustration was defined as interference with a goal *response,* thus keying frustration to an objective barrier or difficulty, and to manifest behavior.[2] Interference was felt to be through punishment or goal inaccessibility, further confusing frustration as blockage with frustration as deprivation.[3]

On this conceptual base, the Yale group put forward its famous assumption (Dollard et al., 1939:1):

> This study takes as its point of departure the assumption that *aggression is always a consequence of frustration.* More specifically the proposition is that the occurrence of aggressive behavior always presupposes the existence of frustration and, contrariwise, that the existence of frustration always leads to some form of aggression.

They further hypothesized a direct positive proportionality between the instigation to aggression and the amount of frustration. This amount depended on the strength of the drive toward a goal, the degree of interference, and the number of frustrated responses. The resulting instigation to aggression will be directed toward the perceived agent of frustration (displacement), and the act of aggression reduces instigation to aggression (catharsis).

This formulation, which hardly stood up to theoretical and conceptual analysis, was operationally precise and, although it assumed internal drives, it was in the stimulus-response, behavioral tradition. It generated considerable laboratory experimentation[4] and empirical research.

More than two decades of research[5] has shown that frustration does not invariably lead to aggression, that frustration can lead to nonaggression, that aggression can occur without frustration, that in some cultures aggression is not a typical response to frustration, that some situations (such as threat and insult) can evoke more aggression than frustration, that the injustice of frustration is more significant than frustration itself, that frustration subsumes a diverse set of conditions, and that the aggression-frustration linkage need not be innate and could be learned. What began as an exciting statement of a psychophysical law has ended with a conclusion that should have been anticipated: frustration sometimes provokes aggression; and aggression is sometimes provoked by frustration.

> The widespread acceptance of the frustration-aggression notion is perhaps attributable more to its simplicity than to its predictive power. In point of fact, the formula that frustration breeds aggression does not hold up well under empirical scrutiny in laboratory studies in which conditions regarded as frustrative are systematically varied. . . . [F]rustration, as commonly defined, is only one—and not necessarily the most important—factor affecting the expression of aggression. [Bandura, 1973:33]

Qualifications not withstanding, social scientists, influenced by the frustration-aggression hypothesis, have often made it an assumption in social analysis and theories of relative deprivation. I now turn to these.

3.2 RELATIVE DEPRIVATION

It is remarkable that those who are most deprived, most oppressed, most in need, are not those who usually violently rebel. Of course there have been food riots and peasant uprisings, but most often revolutions and violence have occurred when conditions are better or have been improving, and among those who are not the most deprived.

Explanations vary but generally focus on two propositions. First, deprivation is subjective, a function of a person's perception, needs, and knowledge. To nail deprivation to an objective or absolute lack of something such as freedom, equality, or sustenance, is to ignore that definitions of these shift according to historical period, culture, society, position, and person.

However, some internal norms or standards, some bench-marks, against which to assess deprivation are still required. The second proposition, therefore, deals with these norms. It asserts that a person takes his presently perceived or expected position, achievements, gratifications, or capabilities as a base of comparison against his wants or needs, or what he feels he ought to have. The gap between wants or oughts and gratifications or capabilities is then a person's deprivation, or *relative* deprivation in the sense that it depends on the individual's base of comparison.

The literature on these two principles and on relative deprivation is well organized in Ted Gurr's *Why Men Rebel* (1970), which merits discussion. The idea of relative deprivation has been used either to measure fairness, inequality, or social justice, or to explain grievance, social hostility, or aggression. Gurr's concern (and mine in considering relative deprivation here) is with relative deprivation as a cause of aggression.

Surely relative deprivation seems to underlie much violence. But granting this, how are the two linked? Relative deprivation is a subjective, unobservable *assessment* of a person. Social and especially political violence, such as guerrilla wars and revolutions, are collective *objective* manifestations. How can the subjective one cause the objective other? Gurr's answer comes in three parts.

First, we must understand relative deprivation as creating the "potential for collective violence " This is because relative deprivation is a frustration that leads to aggression

In summary, the primary source of the human capacity for violence appears to be the frustration-aggression mechanism. Frustration does not necessarily lead to violence, and violence for some men is motivated by expectations of gain. The anger induced by frustration, however, is a motivating force that disposes men to aggression, irrespective of its instrumentalities. If frustrations are sufficiently prolonged or sharply felt, aggression is quite likely, if not certain, to occur. To conclude that the relationship is not relevant to individual or collective violence is akin to the assertion that the law of gravitation is irrelevant to the theory of flight because not everything that goes up falls back to earth in accord with the basic gravitational principle. The frustration-aggression mechanism is in this sense analogous to the law of gravity: men who are frustrated have an innate disposition to do violence to its source in proportion to the intensity of their frustrations . . . [Gurr, 1970:36-37]

To comprehend this assumed connection between frustration and relative deprivation, we must look at Gurr's definitions. Relative deprivation "is defined as actors' perception of discrepancy between their value expectations and their value capabilities" (p. 24). It is the gap between that "to which people believe they are rightfully entitled" and that which "they think they are capable of getting and keeping" (p. 24). It is essential to note that deprivation is not based on wants or needs alone, but on the wants and needs that a person feels he ought to have or deserves. Most of us want a million dollars, but in Gurr's theory few of us will feel that we have been deprived, since we do not believe we are rightfully entitled to this sum. The person denied a promotion he wants and feels he deserves will be deprived; the person denied a promotion he wants but feels he does not deserve will not be deprived.

Rightful entitlement is a normative concept. It assumes some criterion of the justness or fairness of what is due. Therefore, by definition Gurr's notion of relative deprivation links subjective wants and perceived justice on the one hand with perceived capabilities on the other. Frustration then results from inability to gratify just wants. And this frustration creates the potential for collective violence (aggression).

Gurr's whole theory of collective and political violence rests on this single pillar. As this pillar falls, so goes his theory. And it does fall, for these reasons. First, as discussed in the last section and chapter, tests of the frustration-aggression hypothesis have had mixed empirical results, and it was concluded that frustration causes some aggression but also can lead to nonaggression.

Second, man's needs, such as protectiveness, pugnacity, and security, can directly lead to collective aggression. Some deprive themselves greatly to participate in collective violence for higher causes (God, country, freedom); others, for personal glory and esteem or because their friends are involved; still others, to improve their own conditions, to decrease their relative deprivation. Collective violence then may be instrumental, a conscious choice of a means to improve one's lot, not necessarily an automatic, emotional, and irrational aggressive response to frustration.

Third, given the variation between cultures and persons with relation to how frustration is handled and the importance of social learning, Gurr could have assumed that relative deprivation is a potential for collective cooperation. A relatively deprived person may believe that the gap between rightful wants and capabilities is due to evils he committed in a previous life, to God's will, or to his own laziness. He then may determine to live a better, more socially useful life, or to try to improve his capabilities.

Finally, a frustrated person may regress; he may withdraw from human interaction associated with the frustration, absorb it into a higher goal, or try to cope with it.

Gurr should have made relative deprivation and frustration one ingredient in the potential for collective aggression, along with man's needs, character (temperaments), social learning, and interests (goals).[6] How these all are relevant to Gurr's theory is discussed later. First it is important to summarize the remainder of his theory.

Thus initially we have the assumption that relative deprivation causes frustration. The intensity and scope of the frustration in turn lead to the potential for collective violence. The second part of the theory concerns the transformation of this potential into a narrower one for political violence—the "politicization of discontent."

Two variables politically focus the potential for collective violence. The first is the normative justification for political violence. The second is the perceived utility of such violence, based on some past experience. If political violence is believed to be legitimate and has worked in the past or elsewhere, the intensity and scope of these two variables determine the degree to which the potential for collective violence is transformed into the potential for political violence.

The final step in Gurr's theory is the transformation of political potential to political manifestation. Two balance of power variables are responsible for this. One is the balance of dissident to regime coercive control; the other is the balance of dissident to regime institutional support. Political violence is likely to be at its greatest when regime and dissidents have nearly equal power and considerable institutional support.

Thus for Gurr, political violence results from the frustrations of relative deprivation, but only if there is normative and utilitarian justification for violence, and the dissidents' coercive power and institutional support matches the regimes.

Before relating relative deprivation to the conflict helix, some other approaches should be briefly summarized. Considering the historical evidence that revolutions and rebellions do not appear when people are most deprived or oppressed, but when there has been a period of improving conditions, Davies (1962, 1969, 1970, 1973) has proposed a "J-curve" theory of political violence.

First, between what people want and what they get there is usually a gap, which is normally accepted, rationalized, and justified within society. If society is progressing and conditions are improving in some sense, people's wants will increase, but so will gratification. However a sharp downturn in gratifications, such as that due to a sudden economic depression, widens a gap between what people want and get, reversing their expectations of satisfying their wants. Frustration is thereby created, and the probability of violence is increased. Violence "becomes increasingly likely when *any* kind of basic need which has come to be routinely gratified suddenly becomes deprived" (Davies, 1973:247). Deprivation is relative, therefore, to previous gratifications and expectations.

As with Gurr, Davies assumes a frustration-aggression mechanism in connecting deprivation to violence. "Violence is always a response to frustration . . ." (1973:251). And writing about the greater probability of violence inherent in a sudden increase in deprivation, he says: "The psychological basis lies in the frustration of basic needs, a frustration induced by the sudden reversal in gratifications" (1973:246-247). As the frustration-aggression hypothesis falls, so does Davies' theory.

There are a number of differences between the theories of Davies and Gurr (Davies, 1973:248). In particular, Davies emphasizes the time element and sees as crucial not simply a deprivation gap but one resulting from a reversal in gratifications. For Gurr, the gap creates frustration, and he subsumes Davies' theory as a special case (Gurr, 1970:52-54); for Davies, the suddenly increasing gap when improving conditions worsen creates the frustration.

Gurr and Davies notwithstanding, the frustration-aggression hypothesis need not underlie relative deprivation theories. Runciman (1966), for example, has proposed a strictly sociological theory of relative deprivation in which frustration plays no role. Relative deprivation is a sense of inequality resulting from a comparison with some reference group. The choice of this group is crucial, for it would be possible to choose in such a way that one's sense of deprivation, or lack of it, does not reflect objective inequalities. This would explain why the deprived or oppressed often accept their conditions, for if their reference groups are equally oppressed and poor, there is little sense of deprivation. This would also explain the effect of war, social dislocations, communication, and education in stimulating relative deprivation, since these factors tend to change the groups against which people compare themselves.

According to Runciman, the sense of deprivation must be related to the dimensions of inequality existing in society. These he sees as class, status, and power (or in my terms, wealth, prestige, and power). Deprivation along one dimension may not be matched by deprivation along another, nor is actual inequality along a dimension necessarily matched by the sense of deprivation felt. Runciman applied his theory to the relative deprivation of the manual working class in England, both historically and to sample survey data he collected. He found that the magnitude and frequency of relative deprivation in class were seldom correlated with objective class inequalities for manual workers (p. 93). Moreover, their sense of relative deprivation in status has increased while their objective inequality has declined (p. 96).[7] And regarding power, their relative deprivation has declined as the workers' power (through the Labour Party) has increased (p. 121).

In discussing Gurr, Davies, and Runciman, I have only touched on the varied relative deprivation literature;[8] nonetheless the most prominent theories today have been summarized. How then does the idea of relative deprivation relate to the conflict helix?

3.3. INJUSTICE VECTOR

In the simplest view, relative deprivation is the difference between what a person wants and what he gets. For example, a man who fails to get a desired promotion, or a person who wants a higher income are deprived.

A number of difficulties are associated with this definition, however. First, we all have many wants that remain unsatisfied, but we do not feel deprived, frustrated, or angered. I want a better memory, unlimited research funds, a new car, and so on, but lack of these things hardly makes me unhappy. Usually I feel either that the personal cost in terms of other values or wants is too large, or that I do not deserve the benefits, or that it is not right that I have them anyway (such as unlimited research funds). The man who was not promoted may feel that a better person won or that his work so far has not been really deserving. The truly deprived, the very poor and oppressed, may feel that their lowly status is due to God's will or their own faults ("not having studied hard enough," "not having the brains," or not wanting "the greater responsibility"). Thus a wants-get gap may create little strain, tension, frustration, or conflict.

Clearly, the crucial element is a person's subjective evaluation of this gap, of whether his want is something he simply desires, ought to have, is entitled to, or is his right. Thus if one feels he ought to be promoted (by reason of achievement) and is not, or the very poor man feels that society is morally obliged to provide him with basic necessities, the gap between a just want and what the person gets can generate irritation, anger, frustration, and conflict.

But the self may see this gap as being under personal control. That is, he may feel capable of closing the gap, but he may also be unwilling to give up other wants or values to do so. For example, a scientist feeling that he lacks the prestige his work should bring him may be unwilling to go on the lecture circuit, attend the conferences, and write the popularizing books that would make him better known.

Surely, what is involved in the subjective feeling of deprivation is not only a disparity between just wants and gets. Capability also is important, as in Gurr's definition, where deprivation is a gap between just wants (what one feels entitled to) and what one feels capable of getting.

Here also, however, difficulties exist. If one believes he is incapable of overcoming the gap, thus feels deprived, the possibility of rational action is foreclosed. It follows that the greater the relative deprivation, the greater the propensity to political violence only if one assumes such propensity to be a nonutilitarian, nonrational, and emotional reflex. For to lack the capability means that something does not lie within one's perceived ability. It is therefore illogical to bring in utilitarian and rational considerations (as does Gurr) to explain the political violence of the deprived. If through the media of new reference groups, communication, propaganda, and so forth, one reassesses his capability, becomes persuaded that what he ought to have is now within his capability (through, say, harder work, demonstrations, or revolutions), then given the definition of relative deprivation as a gap between just wants and capabilities, the relative deprivation has subjectively disappeared prior to action, and there is no longer a basis for action.

To avoid such problems, we might define "relative deprivation" as a gap between just wants and expected want satisfaction. In other words, the gap between just wants and gets is defined relevant to a future state of affairs. However this definition does not consider the basis of the expectations. The gap may exist because one lacks the capability, or the just-want conflicts with other just wants one prefers to satisfy. In neither case need anger or driving irritation arise.

A general definition that would escape these problems seems to be out of reach—perhaps because of the difficulties of defining objectively both the want and the base of comparison (e.g., capabilities, gratifications, or expectations). For some, deprivation may lie in ungratified just wants alone; for others it may lie both in unsatisfied just wants and in personal lack of capability (say, due to poor education they believe the "system" gave them); and for still others it may be attributed to just wants being unjustly blocked by others and requiring unjust effort to achieve. One way to avoid this problem is to simply consider relative deprivation as a sense generated by a comparison to others. This is Runciman's approach. Then we can focus on the person or group against which the comparison is done and the particular wants involved. Whether the comparison also involves what one has, can have, is capable of getting, or expects, is then bound within the sense of deprivation.

However this approach still shares a problem with the other definitions, the use of the word "deprivation," which stems from "deprive" and denotatively means a state of having something taken away or withheld. This meaning often does not fit the case of "relative deprivation," since a person may want something he has not had, such as more wealth, and no one or no thing may be withholding gratification from him. His own situation, abilities, or lack of will may be responsible for the "deprivation." In this sense, the idea of relative deprivation is already a value-loaded concept, since its application implies something external which is preventing, blocking, or withholding certain valued things.

Compounding this denotative confusion is the connotation of "deprivation" associated with "privation." When deprivation is used, I sense that a person is not only deprived, but deprived of life's essentials. It rubs my sense for the word the wrong way to consider the relative "deprivation" of a rich man suffering a lack of servants, of a movie star who gets only third billing, or of a powerful politician who loses an election. The word seems best applied to the very hungry and needy.

Both connotatively and denotatively, therefore, the concept of deprivation almost unconsciously leads to an emphasis on certain kinds of wants, on the poor versus the wealthy, on the subordinate class versus the superordinate, and on the proletariat versus the bourgeoisie. It is partly for this reason, it seems to me, that those using the term slip from their subjective consideration into a concern for the objective inequalities of the poor and working class. The point is not whether this emphasis is right or wrong, just or unjust. A term meant to cover any gap between *subjective* just wants and what one has, can have, or is capable of getting, should be neutral with respect to the objective nature of those wants. The sense of the term should equally apply to the rich man desiring a bigger yacht, the dictator wanting order, the prisoner craving liberty, the clerk wishing for a promotion, the man coveting another's wife, or the beggar hungering for food. The intensity of "deprivation" felt over the lack of food may be no less than that felt over the lack of additional wealth, power, and so on. Witness the murders and crimes committed by wealthier people and members of the middle class, to gratify an intense desire.

To avoid these problems with the term "deprivation" and with the various definitions of relative deprivation previously discussed, I define the just-want gap as a psychological vector—as an *injustice vector* generated by comparison with others. There are several advantages to this approach.

First, another person or group provides the base of comparison of one's wants and gratification. Surely one can have absolute principles and norms against which to judge wants and gratifications, and just wants unjustly unsatisfied may be judged to be against God or nature. But my concern is with social interaction, with transactions between men, and with social conflict. And for this reason the comparison to others in assessing justice—social justice—is essential.

This definition overcomes another problem in the relative deprivation literature. Usually (with some exceptions, such as Runciman) the perspective is monadic. A person's relative deprivation comes from within; the want gap is an internally produced difference between *a person's* wants and gets, cans, or abilities. Thus interaction and perception of *others* do not play a role at the initiation of deprivation. Once deprivation is produced, however, one may combine with others to be collectively violent or be prevented from expressing discontent by the opposition of others. With my definition, however, interaction with others, society, occurs at the very inception and is bound to this just-want gap.

A second aspect of my definition is that a *vector of power* is involved—a force toward behavior. It is a vector of interests, as I have used this expression throughout, that is generated within man's motivational structure, in relation to needs, other interests, roles, and sentiments such as the superego and man's superordinate goal.

Third, the vector is generated in terms of one's perceived sociocultural distances from others. Here the discussion of distance vectors in previous volumes is relevant, and I simply note the relationship between the injustice vector and these social distances in the psychological field. First consider that interests are vectors of power (activated, energized attitudes) in man's motivational field, a region of the psychological field. The components of this space, man's needs (sex, hunger, security, etc.), provide the energy for the field. Some of the interests cluster into sentiments, of which a particular kind, the superego, forms man's normative interests, his oughts, ethics, and morality. To illustrate, Figure 3.1 presents this field defined by the hunger and self-assertion needs for John, along with two normative vectors of interests, one concerning a belief in man's right to sustenance, and the other a belief that rewards should be proportional to investments (of time, energy, preparation, etc.). An interest is an active "I want something." John's interests are "I want all men to have sustenance" and "I want man to be proportionately rewarded."

Now, assume that John is a struggling, unknown artist, whose *interest* in a sustaining income is represented in Figure 3.2. This interest is related to his superego, specifically to his normative interests as shown. Thus the interest in part reflects a belief in a sustenance right and a belief in merit and, moreover, stems from hunger and self-determination needs, which also contribute to the normative interests.

Just wants are those projections of our interests (wants) on

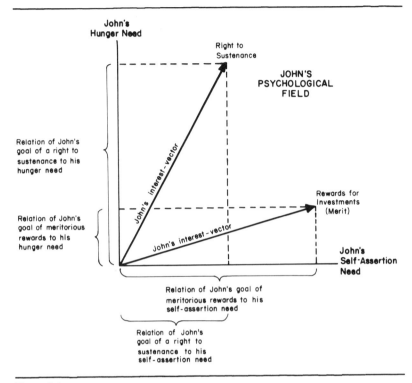

Figure 3.1

the normative vectors. This is shown in Figure 3.2.[9] *Just wants may be less than and different in direction in the psychological field from the pure interest* (which is formed partly by the nonnormative aspects of an individual's needs). For example, the income interest may push simply toward a dishwashing job. But the normative components may push toward either doubling one's efforts to sell more paintings or creating a need for welfare or social security (which is a "right"). So far, we have a just want along two normative vectors, but no *injustice vector.*

Consider now that John becomes acquainted with Arnold, a playboy of inherited wealth who feigns an interest in art. John *perceives* Arnold in his psychological space in terms of a distance between them that is related to John's just wants. This is represented in Figure 3.3. The projections of this distance on the normative interests specify his sense of injustice, with his

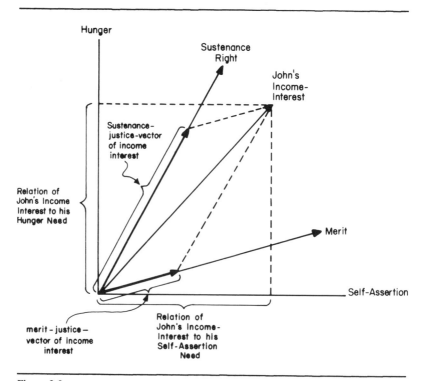

Figure 3.2

just but unsatisfied wants, in comparison to this playboy of "low merit" and inherited wealth. The *injustice vector* is then simply the sum of these projections of the distances onto the normative vectors. It is comparative, related to needs and interests; and as a vector of interest it is a power, a force to action.[10] Moreover, the injustice vector is formed within a person's psychological field relative to his interests and depends partially on his perception of another. And the vector is value neutral. It favors no want. Thus I believe this perspective constituting the injustice vector overcomes many problems in the relative deprivation literature while integrating the concept with the idea of a psychological field and social interaction.

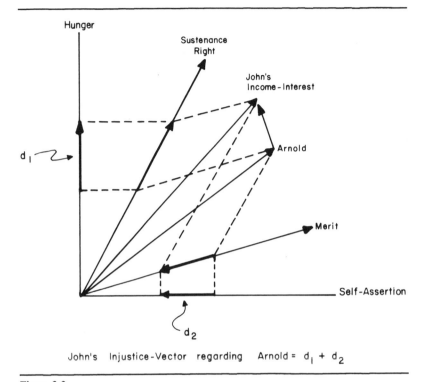

John's   Injustice-Vector   regarding   Arnold = $d_1 + d_2$

Figure 3.3

3.4 AND THE CONFLICT HELIX

The relationship of relative deprivation-turned-injustice vector to the process of conflict is easily clarified. Injustice vectors—the moral sense of deprivation relative to others—are part of the conflict situation. These are vectors of interest, the opposition of which creates the conflict situation. Here, awareness (or perception) and the situation give context and meaning to the opposing interests; expectations of behavioral outcomes interrelate the injustice vector and its drive to action with the capability of the other and our expectation of his behavior. In other words, the situation of conflict involves our interests and their justness; our perception of others and our sense of injustice by comparison; and our beliefs about the capabilities of others and the outcomes of our actions. Within the framework of the helix, the conflict situation comprises the variables important to transforming the potential for collective violence into the potential for class violence and, finally, into manifest violence. At the collective level, the injustice vector fundamentally defines the class consciousness necessary to the class struggle within all organizations, including the state.

The initiation phase of manifest conflict involves a trigger provoking the will to action, and the occurrence of such a mechanism depends on the balance of powers an individual perceives between himself and others. Consequently a sense of injustice is no guarantee of action. This is also true of Gurr's model, in which the transformation of potential to manifestation depends on a balance of power.

But deprivation theory does not explain what happens after the manifest conflict or violence ensues, while the conflict helix is in mid-ascent. Out of manifest conflict a balance is formed among the diverse interests held by people on the basis of their capability and credibility. There ensues adjustment among the diverse vectors of injustice, an adjustment based on subjective perception and expectations honed by the reality of others. Conflict and the resulting balance form a structure of expectations that enables different views of injustice and different classes to live together.

In time these expectations may become incongruent with the underlying balance; a person may develop new reference groups, have new experiences, be the object of an ideological campaign ("workers are oppressed"). The sense of injustice may change such that the previous class balance (between workers and management in a factory) no longer reflects the parties' interests, or the underlying capabilities or credibility of the parties may alter (bureaucratic dissension may weaken governmental control over dissidents). Then a trigger, such as an event provoking a rearoused or newly inflamed sense of injustice may provoke a turn of the conflict helix, a new balancing of powers and injustices, of classes.

In a sense, the conflict helix helps me to answer the question, What is social justice? Just wants and injustice vectors vary considerably among people. Such interests and feelings are diverse, multidimensional, *and personal.* Moreover, the amount willingly sacrificed to satisfy just wants or to right a sense of injustice varies across individuals. People have different capabilities and expectations. And the overriding superordinate goals, self-esteem, and wills are intrinsic to the individual.

Then how *do* we determine what is just? How do we balance? Given the diversity of man, this question can only imply two alternatives: we force *our* view of social justice on someone else (say, through governmental coercion), or people settle for themselves and among themselves their own balance. If the conflict helix as a field process operates at all levels without the imposition of an antifield on it, the diverse views of social justice will compromise and balance in terms of interests, capabilities, and expectations. This argues for the maximum freedom, for a precondition of the conflict helix is that each is free to pursue his just wants and to square his sense of injustice against others. The precondition of social justice is therefore freedom. More on this in the last chapter.

NOTES

1. In more technical language, they provide a cognitive framework, a model, which helps us structure reality.

2. One can be frustrated without behaving, because of anticipated or perceived blocks to one's interests. A goal to ship a new automobile from California to Hawaii may be frustrated by a shipping strike. But if one had taken no prior actions to have an auto shipped, then according to the Yale group, there was no frustration.

To make this concept measurable and testable in the laboratory, frustration was limited by definition to actions already initiated. Research power was thereby gained, but the meaning of frustration in man's life and our understanding of it were distorted.

3. This is one of Fromm's (1973:67) criticisms.

4. Methodological dogma is not to be deterred by facts. Experiments on samples of students cannot possibly involve the range and intensity of frustration or allow the scope and violence of aggression required to test the frustration-aggression hypothesis. Yet rather than looking to history, case studies, or naturalistic observation, researchers in the main followed the example of the Yale group and took to the laboratory.

5. For reviews of the empirical literature, see Buss (1961), Megargee (1972), Berkowitz (1962), Himmelweit (1950), and Yates (1962).

6. Gurr (1969) has tested his theory on cross-national data for 114 nations. He measured relative deprivation as a combination of the intensity and scope of economic and political discrimination, political separation, dependence on foreign economies, lack of educational opportunity, and religious divisions. All these variables are questionable measures of relative deprivation as Gurr defined it.

Education, for example, may lead through greater awareness to more relative deprivation, not less. The combination of these variables measured on a short term correlated .32 with turmoil across nations, .45 with conspiracies, and .47 with total strife; when persisting deprivation is considered, the correlations were .27, .30, and .35. These are all low, but in the positive direction.

Nothing can be concluded from this, however, since Gurr is correlating measures of a *disposition* with a *manifestation*. Within his theory (which does *not* stipulate that the *greater* the relative deprivation, the *greater* the strife), relative deprivation as potential is transformed into violence through a series of intervening variables. Because of this, even negative correlations would not invalidate the theory. Therefore no empirical correlations between deprivation and strife alone would invalidate this assumed relationship.

In a later part of his paper, Gurr regresses strife onto his measures of relative deprivation and of legitimacy, tradition of strife, regime's coercive control, strength of institutions and their facilitation, and accounts for 64% of the variation in total strife. This is a practically and statistically significant result. The result is undermined, however, by the inclusion of variables whose measurement in part depends on the prior existence of civil strife. For example, his independent variables are tradition of civil strife, facilitation (in part "the supplies provided rebels during the 1961-65 period"), and size of regime's forces weighted by loyalty (in part measured by "the length of time since the last forceful intervention of the military and police against the regime, and the frequency with which they resorted to illicit force in the 1961-65 period"). Thus the multiple regression results might be explained by a theory simpler than Gurr's: strife leads to more strife.

The problem with Gurr's tests lies in the distance between his measures and his concept of relative deprivation. A more sensitive test was done by Portes (1974) using sample survey results (which do get at subjective dispositions) from Chilean slums, during 1968-1969. He found differences in expectation of goal fulfillment and subjective frustration to be unrelated to leftist radicalism. Rather than frustration resulting from relative deprivation being crucial, the important variable is "structural blame," the imputation of responsibility to the government or socioeconomic system for perceived deprivation. On structural blame and the secondary importance of relative deprivation, see also Portes and Ross (1974) and Halebsky (1974). The latter is a useful review of the relevant literature.

Incidentally, well worth pondering is Portes' (1974) explanation of the scope and persistence of the belief in relative deprivation as a cause of aggression or radicalism. He sees much of the literature as post factum justification of successful revolution.

7. Incidentally, consistent with the findings discussed in Section 35.2 (Rummel, 1975), he found that education increased the sense of relative deprivation in status (p. 102). This should caution those who assume, in using an aggregate measure of education, that higher educational opportunity means lesser deprivation.

8. For reference to much of this literature, see Gurr (1970, Chapter 2).

9. The manner of geometrically projecting the income-interest vector onto the two normative vectors may be unfamiliar. The two normative vectors are oblique. Therefore the projections on one of the oblique vectors are drawn parallel to the other vector.

10. The vector diagrams with attendant mathematics could be considered to be a mathematical model of Runciman's reference group approach to relative deprivation. I am not sure, however, that Runciman would accept the underlying assumptions of my approach involving vectors of powers, the need components, the calculus of interests and corresponding attitudinal lattice, and the psychological field.

Chapter 4

OTHER PSYCHOLOGICAL CAUSES
AND CONDITIONS

The origin of conflict can be frequently traced to false perception.
Burton, 1968:67

I have discussed the psychological conditions or causes of conflict of much current interest. There remain others that cannot be treated in the same detail, but nonetheless should be mentioned in conjunction with the conflict helix. These are misperception, dissonance, expectations, and righteousness.

4.1 MISPERCEPTION

It is a truism that man sees others through a lens distorted by his own wishes, needs, and experience. Such misperception surely can be a base of conflict, for our actions follow our perceptions, and if we perceive others as evil and act accordingly, we will generate responses in kind. Some, like White (1966), have carried this truism to the highest level, arguing that wars, especially the conflict in Vietnam, are a consequence of misperception. Correct the misperceptions, so the argument goes, and we will have made a gigantic step toward peace and harmony.

Of course this view does not take into account that many conflicts may arise because of entirely accurate perceptions of mutually opposing interests and values. Indeed, I would argue at the international level that until recently United States and

Soviet foreign policy elite knew each other very well and judged accurately their respective antagonistic interests.

The misperception argument, unfortunately, neglects the overwhelming importance of realistic conflicts that are based on an actual clash of interests. The mugger and his victim, the revolutionary and the governor, and the food rioter and the guard are not conflicting because of misperception but because of deeply felt opposing interests. All human behavior is seated in psychological variables, to be sure. But to hang a type of social behavior like conflict on the peg of misperception is to neglect the importance of interests, needs, morality, temperament, and so on, as well as the self, will, and superordinate goal. Perception is an outcome of the confrontation of this field with reality's powers.

If, in fact, misperception is operating, we should focus not on misperception itself but on the operation of the whole field in relation to the specific external forces confronting it. This is done through explicating the process of the conflict helix. Perception plays a role during all phases. Perceptual awareness of another transforms conflict structure into situation, and the perception of another's capabilities, interests, and credibility underlie the instigation to conflict behavior—the balancing of interests.

This balancing is the cauldron within which misperceptions become corrected. It is the test of their reality. Through mutual adjustment, an equilibrium is struck between mutual perceptions of capabilities, credibilities, and opposing interests, and cooperative behavior ensues. But adjustments change and perceptions alter. They may cease to correspond to the reality of the balance. In this sense, these incongruent perceptions are misperceptions that contribute to the breakdown in the structure of expectations. But *such misperceptions are a part of the whole process of conflict.*

Besides neglecting realistic conflicts, the misperception argument wrongly views conflict as wholly undesirable. But it is through conflict that misperceptions are corrected or at least made compatible. Conflict may be harmful, may produce death, injury, and destruction. But conflict also may enable people to live together. It may bind society together.

Conflict is the reality of *other* men, each with his psychological field, his own perceptions, his individual interests. If our misperception of others leads to conflict, the result will be either corrected perceptions or the striking of a balance enabling both parties to accommodate to the viewpoints that produced the conflict.

4.2 COGNITIVE DISSONANCE

Cognitive dissonance was discussed in the previous volume, especially regarding status disequilibrium and its effects. This dissonance is an imbalance between one's perceptions, beliefs, relationships, statuses, and so on, between their negative and positive aspects. It perhaps is best exemplified by the saying: "A friend of my friend is a friend; an enemy of my friend is an enemy." If one has two friends who become enemies, the problem of dissonance arises.

Dissonance provokes field forces that often change perception in order to balance psychological elements. Thus a friend becomes perceived as an enemy, complimentary information about an enemy becomes favorable, or events contrary to one's hopes are perceived as fulfilling the hopes.

Cognitive dissonance and the consequent balancing of perception is a special case of misperception, and it takes field processes into account. And surely cognitive dissonance, especially as it operates for the person with discrepant statuses (see Rummel, 1976, Chapter 18), can provoke conflict. But as with misperception generally, dissonance operates as part of the conflict helix *in its social significance.* Dissonance may create opposing interests and provoke their balancing, and it may be rectified by the process of overt conflict. Moreover, the resulting balance underlying nonconflict interaction may be upset by dissonance psychologically creating imaginary events or misperceptions of interests, capabilities, or credibility.

Dissonance in its effects, like perception, expectations, and the other psychological aspects of man, is part of a field and its processes. We should understand dissonance in relation to the whole that is the conflict helix, rather than comprehend conflict from the operation of dissonance.

4.3 EXPECTATIONS

If man expects aggression, he will behave aggressively; if he expects violence, he will act violently; if he expects war, he will wage war. This is the belief of some who feel that the base psychological cause of violent conflict is the expectation of such conflict. For man will prepare for it, try to anticipate it, and see others in the light of its possibility; thus he will create the satisfaction of his own expectations. In sum, the cause of violence is the expectation of violence.

Expectations are the counterpart of perception. Perception is present oriented. It is what we "see" now of others. Expectation is future oriented. It is what we predict of others based on our perceptions, beliefs, experience, reason, and hopes. It is how we think others will react to our behavior. And if one expects opposition, aggression, or violence to be forthcoming, regardless of whether there is a basis in actuality, he will contribute to bringing about the anticipated condition. What is crucial is what men believe. For belief creates the reality toward which man behaves. In this lies the truth of the argument.

But again, conflict is not a singular event, to die without a trace after the explosion. It is a process within which expectations operate by contributing to conflict inception. Yet expectations do not create opposing interests, and although they have a role in perception (we often perceive that which we anticipate), they are not identical with it. Nor are assessments of another's capabilities and credibility identical with expectations of conflict.

Consequently, these other aspects discipline and limit expectations of conflict. No matter how pessimistic our outlook on man, how much we believe that war and violence characterize human society, how confidently we expect any nation to make war on another for gain or glory, we will not expect Nepal to attack India or Yemen to declare war on the Soviet Union.

Expectations are formed and re-formed in the process of conflict. If they are out of kilter with social reality, the resulting conflict with that reality will adjust them sufficiently to create a balance with others, and to ease cooperative behavior. Nor need the expected violent conflict occur. Social powers come in many forms, and the balancing entailing overt conflict can involve attempts at exchange, persuasion, manipulation, and so on. The social learning process of conflict can move one's expectations of violence toward nonviolent alternatives and adjustment. Such are the lessons of learning theory research (Bandura, 1973) and the consequences of the conflict helix.

4.4 RIGHTEOUSNESS

Social violence, revolution, wars usually have been seen as the outgrowth of a negative or aberrant aspect of man's nature or relations. Selfishness, exploitation, deprivation, misperception, insecurity, frustration, ignorance, or the desire for glory have been nominated separately or together to account for social conflict. What has rarely been mentioned or discussed, however, is the positive aspect of man that contributes to social conflict.

Man is certainly egoistic. His focus is usually on himself, on what will improve or enhance his status, security, independence, glory, and so on. But man is also fraternal. He thinks and acts in terms of what is good for his family group, class, or society. He has a protective need, a drive to improve the welfare of others. The existence of this need has been clearly established in multivariate psychological research (Cattell and Warburton, 1967:157), but few have connected such a need to collective violence.

Arthur Koestler captures an aspect of this need when he pinpoints man's "integrative tendency"—a self-transcending tendency—as the culprit. History's holocausts result from the activities of those who fight in the hope of bettering their group, their nation, or mankind. In Koestler's words:

> The crimes of violence committed for selfish, personal motives are historically insignificant compared to those committed *ad majorum glorian Dei,* out of a self-sacrificing devotion to flag, a leader, a religious faith or a political conviction. Man has always been prepared not only to kill but also to die for good, bad or completely futile causes. And what can be a more valid proof of the reality of the self-transcending urge than this readiness to die for an ideal?

> No matter what period we have in view, modern, ancient, or prehistoric, the evidence always points in the same direction: the

tragedy of man is not his truculence, but his proneness to delusions. "The worst of madman is a saint run mad": Pope's epigram applies to all major periods of history—from the ideological crusades of the totalitarian age down to the rites which govern the life of primates. [Koestler, 1967:234-235]

Another aspect is seen in the notion of righteous indignation, a feeling of injustice, as a cause of violence highlighted by Banfield (1970:190-193) and Lupsha (1971). Righteousness may be personal, to be sure (such as our reaction to an injust slight), but it often involves our feeling about how man should be treated. A central ingredient in class struggle (in my terms), for example, is a pervasive feeling of righteousness about one's class slogans—political formulas—for resolving man's problems, and a feeling of indignation, of moral outrage, at the treatment of other men, whether of management by strikers or dissidents by government, of workers by capitalists or of the poor by the rich. Our indignation and righteousness are linked to a concern for our fellow man, an altruism basic to humanity.

How does such a fraternal need link into the conflict helix? Needs provide the potential of the conflict structure; their activation and the consequent energizing of connected interests (not wanting a person to suffer for lack of food, to be jailed arbitrarily, or to be shot because of his race or class) partly determine the conflict situation. To know that others are atheists, communists, fascists, or capitalists may be sufficient to focus indignation on them, to interpret the defeat of their interest as a victory for man's progress and justice. In other words, our protective need links to interests specifying the sociopolitical acts or conditions that will improve the welfare of man, and casting particular blame on other groups, individuals, or the other classes for depriving man of this welfare. Focused blame connected to a political slogan is a potent situation of conflict. It is in partially defining this situation that fraternal righteousness (as opposed to the egoistic variety[1] plays a role.

But righteousness is not the preserve of one party to a conflict. All parties may feel that they have justice and God on their side and that man's welfare sits on their shoulders. Moral conflicts are so intense and bitter because all sides sincerely feel that they are right, that what *they* are doing will better mankind. A defeat for their ideas is a defeat of man. "God protect us against crusaders" is no empty slogan.

The balancing of power determines who is right, what justice will prevail. A balance that is struck will enable contradictory indignations to live side by side until time and experience erode their more aggressive and inconsistent aspects or an internal weakening of one of the faiths creates a fertile ground for new conflict.

N O T E

1. The egoistic-fraternal distinction is also used by Runciman (1966). Fraternal deprivation is that felt for one's class (e.g., workers), and one desires to eliminate it for the class. Egoistic deprivation is felt by the self (e.g., when one is denied a raise in pay), and the person desires to improve his condition alone.

PART II

CONFLICT IN
SOCIOCULTURAL PERSPECTIVE

Contradiction and conflict not only precede unity but are operative in it at every moment of its existence. . . . There probably exists no social unit in which convergent and divergent currents among its members are not inseparably interwoven. . . .

Conflict is designed to resolve divergent dualisms; it is a way of achieving some kind of unity. . . . Conflict itself resolves the tension between contrasts.

Georg Simmel, 1955

Chapter 5

MARXISM AND CLASS CONFLICT

This much, at least, we should have learnt from Hegel and Marx: we can only make a contribution to the understanding of consensus, conflict and power by approaching our subject matter critically. A situation characterized by the absence of manifest social conflict may contain important latent conflicts of interest; the latter may have a relatively great potential to serve as the focus of crystallization of manifest conflicts. This being the case we cannot, in sociology as in peace research, direct our attention exclusively to what "is": we must at least be equally concerned with that which "could be."

de Kadt, 1965:471

One of the most powerful sociological explanations of social conflict is that of Karl Marx, who posited a class struggle between proletariat and bourgeoisie intrinsic to capitalist, industrial society. This notion is powerful in being dynamic, intuitively persuasive, and appearing to fit well with current events. It is powerful in providing in one package a description, an explanation, and a prediction of contemporary problems, and a remedy. In outlining this view of social conflict and relating it to the conflict helix, I try to show that the conflict helix agrees with Ralf Dahrendorf's "revisions" of Marx and generalizes Dahrendorf's own theory to all societies.

5.1 MARX AND CLASS CONFLICT

It is important to recognize that Marx viewed the structure of society in relation to its major classes, and the struggle between them as the engine of change in this structure. His was no equilibrium or consensus theory. Conflict was not deviational within society's structure, nor were classes functional elements maintaining the system. The structure itself was a derivative of and ingredient in the struggle of classes. His was a conflict view of modern (nineteenth century) society.

The key to understanding Marx is his class definition.[1] A class is defined by the ownership of property. Such ownership vests a person with the power to exclude others from the property and to use it for personal purposes. In relation to property there are three great classes of society: the bourgeoisie (who own the means of production such as machinery and factory buildings, and whose source of income is profit), landowners (whose income is rent), and the proletariat (who own their labor and sell it for a wage).

Class thus is determined by property, not by income or status. These are determined by distribution and consumption, which itself ultimately reflects the production and power relations of classes. The social conditions of bourgeoisie production are defined by bourgeois property. Class is therefore a theoretical and formal relationship among individuals.

The force transforming latent class membership into a struggle of classes is *class interest.* Out of similar *class situations,* individuals come to act similarly. They develop a mutual dependence, a community, a shared interest interrelated with a common income of profit or of wages. From this common interest classes are formed, and for Marx, individuals form classes to the extent that their interests engage them in a struggle with the opposite class.

At first, the interests associated with land ownership and rent are different from those of the bourgeoisie. But as society matures, capital (i.e., the property of production) and land ownership merge, as do the interests of landowners and bourgeoisie. Finally the relation of production, the natural opposition between proletariat and bourgeoisie, determines all other activities.

As Marx saw the development of class conflict, the struggle between classes was initially confined to individual factories. Eventually, given the maturing of capitalism, the growing disparity between life conditions of bourgeoisie and proletariat, and the increasing homogenization within each class, individual struggles become generalized to coalitions across factories. Increasingly class conflict is manifested at the societal level. Class consciousness is increased, common interests and policies are organized, and the use of and struggle for political power occurs. Classes become political forces.

The distribution of political power is determined by power over production (i.e., capital). Capital confers political power, which the bourgeois class uses to legitimatize and protect their property and consequent social relations. Class relations are political, and in the mature capitalist society, the state's business is that of the bourgeoisie. Moreover, the intellectual basis of state rule, the ideas justifying the use of state power and its distribution, are those of the ruling class. The intellectual-social culture is merely a superstructure resting on the relation of production, on ownership of the means of production.

Finally, the division between classes will widen and the condition of the exploited worker will deteriorate so badly that social structure collapses: the class struggle is transformed into a proletarian revolution. The workers' triumph will eliminate the basis of class division in property through public ownership of the means of production. With the basis of classes thus wiped away, a classless society will ensue (by definition), and since political power to protect the bourgeoisie against the workers is unnecessary, political authority and the state will wither away.

In sum, there are six elements in Marx's view of class conflict.

(1) Classes are authority relationships based on property ownership.

(2) A class defines groupings of individuals with shared life situations, thus interests.

(3) Classes are naturally antagonistic by virtue of their interests.

(4) Imminent within modern society is the growth of two antagonistic classes and their struggle, which eventually absorbs all social relations.

(5) Political organization and power is an instrumentality of class struggle, and reigning ideas are its reflection.

(6) Structural change is a consequence of the class struggle.

Marx's emphasis on class conflict as constituting the dynamics of social change, his awareness that change was not random but the outcome of a conflict of interests, and his view of social relations as based on power were contributions of the first magnitude. However, time and history have invalidated many of his assumptions and predictions. Capitalist ownership and control of production have been separated. Joint stock companies forming most of the industrial sector are now almost wholly operated by non-capital-owning managers. Workers have not grown homogeneous but are divided and subdivided into different skill groups. Class stability has been undercut by the development of a large middle class and considerable social mobility. Rather than increasing extremes of wealth and poverty, there has been a social leveling and an increasing emphasis on social justice. And finally, bourgeois political power has progressively weakened with growth in worker-oriented legislation and of labor-oriented parties, and with a narrowing of the rights and privileges of capital ownership. Most important, the severest manifestation of conflict between workers and capitalist—the strike—has been institutionalized through collective bargaining legislation and the legalization of strikes.

These historical events and trends notwithstanding, the sociological outlines of Marx's approach have much value. His emphasis on conflict, on classes, on their relations to the state, and on social change was a powerful perspective that should not be discarded. The spirit, if not the substance, of his theory is worth developing.

5.2 DAHRENDORF'S CLASS AND CLASS CONFLICT

The ideas of Marx spawned a rich literature; much of it is polemical and political, but some authors have tried to avoid the historical or empirical errors Marx committed, to learn from changes since his time, and to apply the spirit of his sociology to contemporary industrial society. The best of these efforts is Ralf Dahrendorf's *Class and Class Conflict in Industrial Society* (1959).

Dahrendorf recognizes two approaches to society, which he calls the Utopian and the Rationalist. The first emphasizes equilibrium of values, consensus, and stability; the second revolves around dissension and conflict, the latter being the mover of structural change. Both are social perspectives; neither is completely false, but each views a separate face of society. Unfortunately, he feels, the consensus view has dominated contemporary sociology, especially in the United States, and he sets out to create some balance between the two views by developing and illustrating the theoretical power of a class-conflict perspective.

He begins as he must with a review of Marx's writings, a clarification of his model, a discussion of the sociopolitical changes since Marx. A review of subsequent theoretical works bearing on class is followed by a sociological critique of Marx. These necessary scholarly chores completed, Dahrendorf presents his own view of class.

He sees Marx's defining characteristic of class (as property ownership) as a special case of a more general authoritative relationship. Society grants the holders of social positions power to exercise coercive control over others. And property ownership, the legitimate right to coercively exclude others from one's property, is such power. This control is a matter of authority, which Dahrendorf defines, according to Weber, as the probability that a command with specific content will be obeyed by certain people. Authority is associated with a role or position and differs from power, which Dahrendorf claims is individual. Authority is a matter of formal legitimacy backed by sanctions. It is a relation existing between people in impera- tively coordinated groups, thus originating in social structure.

Authority, however, is dichotomous; there is always an authoritative hierarchy on one side and those who are excluded on the other. Within any imperative group are those who are superordinate and those who are subordinate. There is an arrangement of social roles comprising expectations of domi- nation or subjugation.

Those who assume opposing roles have structurally generated contradictory interests, to preserve or to change the status quo. Incumbents of authoritative roles benefit from the status-quo, which grants them their power. Those toward whom this authoritative power is exercised, and who suffer from it, however, are naturally opposed to this state of affairs.

Superordinates and subordinates thus form separate quasi-groups of shared latent interests. On the surface, members of these groups and their behavior may vary considerably, but they form a pool from which conflict groups can recruit members. With leadership, ideology, and the political (freedom) and social conditions of organization being present, latent interests become manifested through political organizations and conflict.

How does Dahrendorf define social classes? They are latent or manifest conflict groups arising from the authority structure of imperative coordinated organizations. Class conflict then arises from and is related to this structure. The structural source of group conflict lies in authoritative domination and subjugation; the object of such conflict is the status quo; and the consequence is to change (not necessarily through revolution) social structure.

It should be stressed that Dahrendorf's theory is not limited to "capitalist" societies. Since authoritative roles are the differentia between classes, classes and class conflict also exist in communist or socialist societies. Classes exist insofar as there are those who dominate by virtue of legitimate positions (such as the Soviet factory manager, party chief, commune head, or army general) and those who are habitually in subordinate positions (the citizen, worker, peasant).

5.3 AND THE CONFLICT HELIX

The Conflict Helix (Chapter 5, pp. 28-29), which describes my view of class conflict as part of the social conflict process, reveals many similarities between the conflict helix and the dynamic perspectives of Marx and Dahrendorf. This section makes these similarities and some of the differences explicit.

The conflict helix begins analytically with a conception of the social space as a field of meanings, values, norms, statuses, and class, where status has the joint meaning of formal positions (as in authoritative roles) and the informal statuses of wealth, power, and prestige. Marx and Dahrendorf also have beginning analytic conceptions of society. For Marx, it is people distributed on the bases of differentiated property ownership and sources of income; for Dahrendorf, it is differential power, norms, and roles.[2]

My notion of social space incorporates power and norms and formal roles, while making explicit the function of cultural meanings and values. This subjective culture is purposely ignored by Dahrendorf in his desire to emphasize the conflict dynamics of society. The existence of some shared meanings and values is a prerequisite of class conflict, however, and a breakdown of crystallized meanings, values, and norms can itself generate the conditions for class conflict. A culture in which slave labor is generally believed right, proper, and sanctioned by the gods, as in classical Greece, will have little associated class conflict.

For Marx, meanings, values, and norms were themselves a product of property relations. Property relations define social space; the conditions of ownership of capital, land, or one's labor constitute dichotomous components distributing individuals in their social relations. The concepts of culture, of subjective meanings, values, and norms were not part of Marx's intellectual world. Their closest counterpart, ideas, were a manifestation of class division.

In the helix, the social space is transformed into a structure of conflict insofar as differential locations in the space define opposing attitudes. For me, an attitude is a psychological disposition to want certain goals. Attitudes form a switchboard between needs and active interests; the connections are wired through acculturation, socialization, and personal learning, and experience. It is the reflection of our culture and society, of our social space. These opposing attitudes are more than simply conflicting wishes or wants; instead we have a clash of opposing perspectives. The structure of conflict defines latent conflict groups, in the sense that people who have opposing attitudes are reservoirs for opposing interests groups.

Now, I define class according to the relationship of people to authoritative hierarchies in groups. There are two classes, those with authoritative roles and those without, and these classes define opposing attitudes (i.e., a particular structure of conflict). Other structures of conflict are not associated with classes, but this is the main one manifested in societal or collective conflict and political struggle.

My view is close to Dahrendorf's. Classes are latent interest groups associated with the authoritative roles of imperatively coordinated organizations. However, Dahrendorf does not distinguish types of groups or dissociate authority and coercion, nor does he deal with the psychological implications of latent interests, feeling it sufficient to treat interests as a sociological category. With this I disagree; for an understanding of the meaning and process of conflict requires a preliminary consideration of perception, expectations, dispositions, needs, and power. To provide such a foundation was the intent of *The Dynamic Psychological Field* (Rummel, 1975) and my treatment of field and power, *The Conflict Helix.*

Aside from the different definitions of class, Dahrendorf and Marx have similar views of latent interests and the class situation. Marx saw classes in relation to property, and this relation defined different life situations and opposing latent interests. No manifest conflict behavior might occur. Indeed, members of opposing classes might interact as though no opposing interests existed. Thus similar class situations are a necessary but not a sufficient condition for manifest struggle, as is also true in the conflict helix.

For Dahrendorf and Marx, as in the conflict helix, awareness of opposition and the activation of interests transforms latent interests into a new situation, one of class consciousness. In the helix, interest is transformed into a conflict situation that is generated by propaganda, contact, communication, leadership, and so on. For Marx and Dahrendorf the transformation is similarly produced. The important point is that in all three views, class consciousness is not automatic but is engendered by some event (e.g., contact), agent (e.g., a leader), or cognitive transformation (e.g., class propaganda).

For Marx and Dahrendorf, however, the conflict situation (my term) implies manifest conflict. Consciousness is equated with struggle. In the helix, consciousness is but a phase toward struggle. No manifest conflict may occur; for the other side may be too strong, the sanctions too severe, or the inertia of habitual interaction patterns too great. In the helix a balance of powers between opposing class interests may be wholly on the psychological level.

Moreover, Marx and Dahrendorf ignore the inception phase of class conflict—the need for a trigger, for will, for preparations, even if psychological. Thus both stress group organization as intrinsic to class conflict; but organization, which is part of the inception phase, is not clearly delimited from a situation of conflict and actual conflict. In some societies preparations may last for years, while workers stock arms, organize cells, and spread the word. On the surface all is stable; underneath a transformation from class consciousness to overt conflict is underway.

Class struggle or conflict, the active opposition of classes, is of course the meat of class theories. The utilization and importance of political power in the struggle is also recognized. Moreover, the three theories equally recognize the importance of the superimposition of class interests in contributing to the intensity of the struggle. Marx puts this in terms of the generalization of separate factory-specific class conflicts, and the increasing homogenization of classes; Dahrendorf refers to the superimposition of role incumbents, such that the same people are generally in the same authoritative relationship across organizations. I treat superimposition in the same manner.

Conflict leads to balance and a structure of expectations; and this is where Marx, Dahrendorf, and the conflict helix diverge. For Marx, class conflict in conjunction with correlated processes (such as increasing worker poverty) leads to the intensification of the dominance of one class, and eventually the disruption of the class society. Revolution brings the proletariat to power, classes are eliminated, and the state that was necessitated to protect the bourgeoisie, gradually disappears. For Dahrendorf, class conflict is a lever of change. The direction of change is indeterminate, except to say that the alteration in social structure is a re-forming of authoritative roles. There is a note of continuous flux here, of balances and new balances. In the helix, the outcome of the struggle is explicit. It is a structure of expectations regulating social interaction, based on a balance among class interests, capabilities, and credibility. But the notion of this structure as the equilibrium of values and norms, as a consensual stability, is missing in Dahrendorf. Moreover, this phase as a momentary stasis, one that can grow out of concordance with the underlying balance and itself be disrupted in new overt class conflict, is a perspective unique to the helix.

At the philosophical level, the three theories share an emphasis on change, power, and conflict. Men are seen in conflict, society as a consequence of this conflict, and social change as produced by struggle. Both Marx and Dahrendorf, however, particularize their theories to class conflict, whereas in the helix, class conflict is but the most severe form of social conflict, and class opposition is only one form of opposition among attitudes and interests. All social conflicts are regarded as involving the same conflict process—the conflict helix.

5.4 A NOTE ON STATUS

Sociologists, especially Americans, have come close to Marxist thinking on conflict in relation to status. Some feel that status-oriented analyses provide a meaninful theory of class conflict that supersedes the Marxist view.[3] It may be useful, therefore, to clarify the role of status within the helix.

For Marx, status, such as wealth or prestige, was usually but not necessarily the outcome of property ownership. Capitalists tended to be wealthy, powerful, and prestigious, and workers were quite the opposite. Statuses contributed to defining the class situation but were not an essential characteristic of it.

Status, moreover, is continuous. There are no clear defining breaks, except perhaps the arbitrary high-low status differentiation. Class is dichotomous, however. It is defined relative to property for Marx, and to authority in Dahrendorf's theory and my view; class and status are correlated, but this correlation does not define class.

Class conflicts are generated by social relations based on

class. Correlated status differences may contribute to this class conflict, or crosscutting status differences may bleed off class tension. *Status is an intermediary variable.*

Status differences generate a structure of conflict, to be sure. As I argued in *The Conflict Helix* (Chapter 18), people are oriented in social space by status distances that define opposing attitudes. But the structure of conflict that results from status imbalance and incongruence is largely individual. Clear lines of demarcation are not formed, and conflict groups do not recruit members from balanced versus imbalanced statuses. Rather, the conflict or interest groups that traverse society are formed out of classes, out of the antagonistic attitudes supporting and opposing the status quo.

The confusion here is that those of high status generally support the status quo; those of low status oppose it. Moreover, those of imbalanced statuses generally oppose the status quo, which contributes to their imbalance. They provide leadership and organization. But to emphasize status as a source of pervasive political conflict is to miss the underlying structure, the latent attitudes from which status differences gain their strength. This underlying structure is whether one legitimately commands or obeys.

5.5 A NOTE ON PROPERTY AND AUTHORITY

Marx highlighted the role of property ownership, whether of land or the means of production, in dominance and power. Historically, he saw primary social relations, culture, and ideology as reflecting property relationships. Moreover, political power, the state, was the instrument for maintaining and protecting property relations, and in mature capitalist society, the business of the state was that of the bourgeoisie.

If property were central, what was the effect of the gradual separation between property ownership and control or management that was occurring in Marx's time through joint-stock companies? For some, like Dahrendorf, this trend presaged the gradual transformation of capitalism into a postcapitalist society dominated by managed corporations and bureaucrats. Even in his own time Marx recognized the joint-stock company as significantly altering the nature of the class struggle. Others, like Zeitlin (1973), argue that Marx recognized the separation of ownership and control as simply a transformation in capitalism, realizing that those who control do so in the name of the capitalists and share their class interests. A position on this controversy need not be taken here. At issue is whether it is authority or property relations that provide the most basic vehicle for understanding class conflict.

Property is that over which one legitimately exercises exclusive control. It is a right granted by society (i.e., the state) to authoritatively exercise sovereignty over the property: to exclude others from it or to regulate them in its use. That property which is socially significant establishes a relationship of domination and subordination among people (e.g., property in slaves, in land or resources, or in capital).

Of course property as sovereign control can be that which man can establish and protect with his own power. But with the growth of society, socially significant property is no longer a matter of personal strength, but of law. It is the power of the state that protects and grants exclusive authority. Thus property has no meaning in society except as defined in the state's law-norms. In essence, then, property ownership is an authoritative role; relations of property, as between worker and factory owner, are relations of authority at the state level.

It is partially for these reasons that class conflicts emerging from such authoritative roles are struggles over state power. For ultimately, the class that controls the state controls property rights.

But property rights, again, are command and control over property. Thus even if property is legally vested in shareholders who grant managers the right to control the company, the managers still exercise command over property, thus stand in a state-sanctioned, authoritative relationship to workers. The separation of ownership and control makes no difference with respect to the locus of authority and the resulting class conflict and struggle.

It follows that the creation of public property, whether nationalized industry or public lands, does not alter the social relationships creating classes and class conflict. Property "owned by the people" is controlled by a few bureaucrats or managers who are given by the state authoritative control over the property. Authoritative roles exist, although their supporting rhetoric is altered, and the superordinate and the subordinate, those commanded and those who obey, still form the stuff of class. Nationalization eliminates socially effective private property; it does not eradicate authoritative control over property and thus over people.

To say that history is the course of property relations breeding power struggles between classes is to confuse universal history with a concrete manifestation in private ownership. Rather, history is the course of authoritative relations breeding power struggles of classes over the status quo. It is a conflict helix—a process of struggle and balance, of historically momentary structures of expectation within which classes coexist; there are periods of social peace, of incremental social change in adjustment to shifts in the underlying balance, of increasing incongruence with the changing class situations, power, and interests, and of social disruption as conflict and possibly violence throughout society serve to create a new balance of authority.

NOTES

1. Marx did not write his intended final chapter in *Capital* on "The Classes." Throughout his writing, however, Marx's observations, comments, and theoretical points provide sufficient detail to patch together the probable structure of his overall argument. This Dahrendorf has done (1959, Chapter 1), and I rely on his interpretation.

2. This comes out most clearly in Dahrendorf's essays (1968).

3. For my analysis of status and coverage of the status literature, see Rummel (1976, Chapters 17-18).

Chapter 6

SAME AND OTHER;
SIMILARITY AND DIFFERENCE

And so iron will be mingled with silver, and brass with gold, and hence there will arise dissimilarity and inequality and irregularity, which always and in all places are causes of hatred and war.

Plato, *The Republic*

6.1 LIKES ATTRACT; UNLIKES REPEL

Consider the following sociological belief. Likes attract; birds of a feather flock together; or, in the words of the ancient Greek poets,[1]

> God is ever drawing like towards like,
> and making them acquainted.

The belief that similars attract, and its corollary, that opposites repel, has constituted a basic sociological explanation for love, friendship, solidarity, and affiliation, while the interaction of opposites has provided the basis for antagonism, hostility, strife, and conflict. Moreover, this belief became in early philosophy a general metaphor for explaining such puzzles as action at a distance (as of the moon on the tides) and magnetism, and in the hands of such ancient philosophers as Heraclitus became a cosmology. Indeed, down to our day, we continue to apply the basic concepts of attraction and repulsion to physical forces, and opposites or contradictions still play a strong role in some contemporary philosophies, as well as in the conflict helix.

However the simple notion that likes attract has not been universally accepted. In *Lysis* (213-223), Plato investigated whether friends were alike, or similarly good or congenial, and through the words of Socrates concluded "If neither the beloved, nor the loved, nor the like, nor the unlike, nor the good, nor the congenial, nor any other of whom we spoke–for there were such a number of them that I cannot remember all–if none of these are friends, I know not what remains to be said."

Hesiod, however, neither accepted that likes attract nor that the question was unresolved. Rather, he argued that likes repel. "Potter quarrels with potter, bard with bard, beggar with beggar" (*Lysis*, 215).

Although some have argued that unlikes attract and likes repel, sociological thought down to the present day has assumed that similarity is a cause of love, friendship, and solidarity, and the notion is incorporated in a variety of works. For example, James Davis (1966:82) posits "The more similar *Person* is to *Other*, the more *Person* will like *Other*." Or, stipulates Heider (1958:186) "p dissimilar to o induces p dislikes o; p tends to dislike a person different from himself." There is no need to multiply these examples, for the assumption can be found throughout contemporary literature.

And the assumption that likes attract has not gone without examination. Beginning with Plato, other philosophers such as Aristotle[2] and Aquinas[3] have subjected the question to analysis. And modern social scientists have empirically tested the notion that similarity causes or underlies love, friendship, or solidarity.[4]

6.2 SIMILARITY AND DISSIMILARITY; SOLIDARITY AND ANTAGONISM

The best contemporary sociological analysis of the belief that likes attract and consideration of the evidence pro and con is Sorokin's chapter "The Roles of Similarity and Dissimilarity in Social Solidarity and Antagonism," in his comprehensive *Society, Culture, and Personality* (1969). A summary of Sorokin's perspective and his conclusion will be helpful at this point, for his analysis is congenial to the understanding I am trying to develop.

Sorokin begins by pointing out three major theories on the question. One is that similarity between people leads to expressions of solidarity, such as marriage, or friendship; another, that dissimilarity leads to solidarity, as in the notion that unlikes attract; and finally, that both similarity and dissimilarity lead to solidarity.[5] The latter includes theories of Durkheim, Tönnies, and MacIver, which divide solidarity into mechanical versus organic,[6] gemeinschaft versus gesellschaft,[7] community versus association.

Sorokin then considers the theory that similarity leads to solidarity in its most popular, contemporary manifestation: that like marries like. His survey of the empirical evidence tends to support this view. Generally, mates seem to be more alike than different.

But the evidence shows only a tendency, and as Sorokin notes, there is even reason to question this. First, the correlations between marriage and similarity are low. Second, the findings are not consistent regarding what constitutes similarity. The traits in one study related to marriage may be uncorrelated or negative in others. Third, in some studies marriage is related to dissimilarity, not similarity. Finally, these studies involve many arbitrary methodological assumptions and judgments. These considerations indicate to Sorokin that the empirical evidence hardly confirms the theory that similarity leads to solidarity.

Characteristically Sorokin, not content to rest on an empirical survey, uses it to introduce an analysis of the theory. He observes that those who have empirically investigated whether likes attract have not analyzed the meaning of "like." Perhaps similar people marry simply because they live close together; their choice is limited by physical distance. Since neighborhoods tend to be homogeneous in racial, religious, and socioeconomic characteristics, within this arena of choice marriages, by chance, would tend to be among likes. No mystical special attraction of likes need be postulated.

Moreover, propinquity is not the only factor in choice. Surely language, status, and race also limit or pattern interaction, thus serve as natural channels for one's choice of mate. Not similarity per se, but whom one meets makes for marriage.

Sorokin's point is a good one, but more recent studies have compensated for this to some extent. For example, a study of marriage patterns in Hawaii (Parkman and Sawyer, 1967) shows that those who are similar in racial-ethnic-cultural backgrounds tend to marry each other, in spite of a considerable mixing of racial-ethnic-cultural types (Japanese, Chinese, Korean, Okinawan, Filipino, Portuguese, Hawaiian, and so on) within the same neighborhoods, schools, and occupations, and similar language and status.

Regardless of these influences on choice, for Sorokin similarity itself seems to play little overall role in the happiness of a marriage. For some occupational groups, similarity seems important, whereas dissimilarity is significant for others. What may be most important for the happiness and the success of a marriage is the similarity in attitudes between the partners, but the evidence on this is inconsistent.

As final one-two punches, Sorokin argues that the universal taboos against marriages between close relations would not make sense if similarity were the crucial element in choice of mate and subsequent happiness. Moreover, marriages are usually between members of opposite sexes, important evidence against the theory that likes attract. Sexual differences, as any husband or wife knows, entail a wide range of physiological, emotional, and behavioral differences.[8]

Sorokin finally concludes that he must reject the theory that likes marry. And in consideration of the evidence and the foregoing points, he also rejects the opposite theory that dissimilarity leads to solidarity.

I must agree. I would soften the negative conclusion somewhat by saying that the sociocultural evidence and empirical studies do not substantiate nor invalidate the idea that similarity or dissimilarity underlies solidarity or antagonism. Our knowledge is inconclusive. I say this without accepting in total Sorokin's line of attack. For his analysis can be faulted for considering the meaning of similarity in a superficial way. But I return to this later.

Having cleared the terrain of false theories, Sorokin examines the theory that similarity and dissimilarity in combination underlie solidarity. Evidence for this is found in the observation that friends generally show a mixture of similar and dissimilar characteristics. The empirical tests of the relationship of similarity alone to friendship reveal that traits are mixed in their contribution. Moreover, marriage seems to require some dissimilarity (in sex and related characteristics) but some similarity in attitudes (toward children, handling money, etc.).

What is the nature of similarity and dissimilarity in general? After all, there are many different kinds, and all are not equally important or, in Sorokin's terms, virulent. No one characteristic by itself, whether age, race, height, weight, or education appears to generate solidarity or antagonism. For example, religion may be a central element in solidarity in some societies at some times, as in Europe in the Middle Ages; or it may be almost an irrelevant characteristic, as in contemporary Japan. What *is* virulent as a similarity or difference depends on the importance society attaches to that quality. A characteristic receives its virulence from the values attached to it by those involved.

Sorokin's point, central in his overall sociology, is that there are no objectively important things. Objective reality becomes socioculturally significant through man's meanings, values, and norms. No objective dissimilarities or similarities can have significance, *sui generis,* in generating solidarity or antagonism. Man must imbue characteristics with meaning and weight them with value before they begin to take on importance. Thus there has been inconsistancy in the empirical evidence about which characteristics (e.g., race or religion) are related to marriage or friendship.

Regarding the relation of similarity and dissimilarity to solidarity in general, Sorokin first says that the identity of the characteristics that comprise socially relevant similarity and dissimilarity depends on the sociocultural mentality, on their meanings and values. This constitutes the important similarity.

Second, if the characteristics are unimportant within a system of values, similarities or dissimilarities between them are unrelated to solidarity or antagonism. This particular conclusion goes far beyond Sorokin's analysis and evidence, and is questionable at its foundation. All factors that affect behavior, whether solidarity or antagonism, are not sociocultural. Man has psychological needs, complexes, mechanisms that simply may be unrecognized by our sociocultural mentality. Aggressiveness as a complex of self-assertion and pugnacity needs and dominance and paranoidal temperaments, for example, may have no meaning or value within a culture, being an unconscious psychological disposition that neither the individual nor society recognizes. Yet the difference between two people in this disposition could well influence their interaction. If both are strongly aggressive, antagonism may result. Solidarity may require that one or both parties be characteristically nonaggressive. I am not saying that such is the case, only that Sorokin's characteristic reduction of reality to meanings and values is carried too far.

A third generalization is that an important sociocultural *similarity* generates *solidarity* if (a) the values for all are abundant and sufficient—they can be shared by all, such as God for Christians, pride for patriots, or truth for scholars; (b) the egos of the parties are fused into one "we," as in a family, intimate friendship, or close association (then the gain of one is the gain of the other, and even scarce values are shared); (c) and the relevant norms—standards or rules of conduct—are concordant.

Fourth, *antagonism* is generated by *similarity* if (a) values such as land, status, or food are scarce and the norms are permeated by an egoistic competition and discord; (b) and the norms are discordant and the values (e.g., becoming mayor of Honolulu) cannot be shared by all.

Fifth, if two people have quite *dissimilar* values, and those of one are considered unimportant by the other, *neither solidarity nor antagonism* is generated.

Sixth, *similarity* in values and norms, in the sense that they are considered equally important, generates antagonism if one affirms what the other denies. For example, a communist and an anticommunist may consider the same things to be important; but much of what one cherishes, the other may detest.

A final generalization is that *solidarity* is encouraged if the main values and norms are similar, and the secondary values are supplementary, or at least diverse or neutral. Thus a marriage between those of different races or religions can be solidary as long as the partners' main values are similar and their secondary values and norms are not discordant.

Sorokin then (1969:143) arrives at this basic conclusion about similarity and dissimilarity.

> From the above it follows that the combination of a basic similarity in the main values and a concordance in the norms of the parties concerned, with a supplementary diversity in their secondary values, is the most conducive to solidary relationships, provided the main values are abundant, or are distributed by all the parties involved according to their concordant norms.
>
> *An opposite and diverse character of the values and norms of the parties, when they are considered important (positively or negatively), and in which the parties have no common system of values and norms, is the most conducive to the generation of intense antagonisms.*

Thus Sorokin's analysis: it is sociologically insightful, comprehensive, and properly emphasizes the role of values and norms. Yet is is not complete. A more careful consideration of the nature of similarity and difference is needed. The analysis should include another perspective on these two qualities—that of social distance. And consideration should be given to both the overall sociocultural context—the field—within which similarities and differences take on value and meaning, and a more specific understanding of values and norms.[9]

6.3 SAME AND OTHER

There is always some point of view in which everything is like every other thing. . . .

Plato, *Protagoras*, 331

To say that likes attract, that solidarity is based on similarity, is to imply some meaning of "alike" or "similar." But what is this meaning? To say two people, or things for that matter, are the *same,* is to say what?

In answering, let me first make some distinctions. Consider that two people can be compared with respect to their *qualities* or *quantities.* Now "qualities" refer to the attributes, characteristics, and properties of people. They are the nonquantitative features by which we classify, categorize, and stereotype the profusion of manifestations that are another's field of expression. These qualities are nothing more than the latents underlying the transitory specifics, determinates, and manifestations that I discussed in *The Dynamic Psychological Field* (Chapter 8), such as physical features, mannerisms, habits, and beliefs.

Two people may have similar, but not exactly the same, qualities, such as red hair. Like similar triangles, two people can share the same form but be quantitatively unequal. A baby, a short person, a tall person all can be fat, yet quantitatively they differ considerably. Therefore, of qualities we say that people are *similar* or alike, but not equal or unequal. Thus we categorize people as similarly whites, in spite of the wide quantitative differences (if we were to try to determine their average color with a spectroscope) among them.

Do qualities admit of degree, or can we say only that people are similar and dissimilar? Here there are two kinds of quality: binary and ordinal. Binary qualities are those that one either has or has not. Being alive, being a member of the Democratic Party, being a banker, being a father are all qualities that are either present or absent. There are then only two possibilities in the similarity or dissimilarity of people in their binary qualities, and if dissimilar, there is no question of degree. For example, if there are three people, i, j, and k, and only i is a governor, then i and j, and i and k are dissimilar in the quality of holding the office of governor. We cannot compare these two pairs to see whether one pair has more or less of this quality. Moreover, j and k are similar in that neither is a governor.

However some qualities allow more comparison than just the binary type. People may be compared on the basis of their power, prestige, responsibility, happiness, friendship, dominance, hunger, or beauty. For such qualities, we may be able to order people with regard to each other, so that this fellow is first, that fellow is second, and so on. Of course, we intuitively rank others on many qualities, such as beauty, power, and trustworthiness. And on such qualities when we say two people are similar, we mean that they share the same ranking. But unlike the binary qualities, when we say two people are dissimilar we do admit of some comparisons in dissimilarity. That is, in ranking on power, two people may be dissimilar but still rank close to each other, such as a mayor and a governor, a president and a vice president. Or they may be dissimilar in power and ranked at opposite extremes, like master and slave, general and private, king and serf. The qualities on which we can base comparisons of the dissimilarities of people I call *ordinal.*

Aside from dissimilarity in binary and ordinal qualities, people also can differ in *quantity,* in the amount of some measure that may be taken of them, such as height, weight, age, I.Q., income, years of education, size of home, reading speed, or size of family. On quantities, we say that people are *equal* or unequal.

Inequality clearly implies a degree or specification of an amount on which people can be compared in their inequality (the difference in age between Mary and Jim is ten years). There is a measurable quantitative difference that can be said to be twice as much or three times more than others. This level of specificity is sufficient for our purposes here. I could define quantitative differences entailing merely interval differences as distinct from those comprising a natural underlying zero point, but to no purpose.[10]

We have then qualities and quantities on which people may be respectively similar or dissimilar, equal or unequal. And dissimilarities can be binary or ordinal, and inequalities may differ by some amount or multiple. But the question still involves cutting across these distinctions. On what should two people be compared? On what qualities or quantities should we say they are similar or dissimilar, equal or unequal?

Here we get into the philosophical distinction between essence and accidents. The essence of a person is that which defines what he is. It is that without which he would not be a person, or John, or Catholic, or American. For example, the essence of man may be having reason or morality; the essence of an American may be independence, self-reliance, and a sense of equality. Clearly essence means a thing's nature. Accidents are then the qualities or quantities that are irrelevant to a thing's essence. So to man *qua* man, fingernail length, hair color, weight, power are accidents. They do not define his essence.

Clearly, if we are to compare people, to say they are similar or dissimilar, equal or unequal, we want to compare their essences. We want to compare not the changing, ephemeral manifestations that from one moment to another specify a person, but the invariant underlying latents that constitute you or me. But this brings us no closer to an answer to our question. For I have replaced "What shall we compare?" with "How do we determine essence?"[11] An answer in part goes back to ancient philosophical concern with the nature of genus and species[12] and in part to the more modern twist given this concern by William James in his treatment of discrimination and comparison in Chapter 13 of *The Principles of Psychology* (1890).

First, the essence of something constitutes that which all such things have in common. Whatever is the essence of man, of social interaction, of conflict, is shared by all men, all social interaction, and all conflict. It was this essence, for example, of all social interaction that was my concern in Chapter 9 of *The Conflict Helix*, where I argued that all social interactions share an orientation toward others.

Second, what is accident is something unique, like a man's biography, a car's rust spots, or a painting's detail. We have here the now-familiar distinction between manifest and latent, but I want to pursue this distinction in a slightly different language more appropriate to our immediate concern.

We find that people are similar on one binary quality, dissimilar on another one, similar on this ordinal quality, dissimilar on that, and dissimilar in varying amounts on certain quantities. Indeed, in looking over the variety of qualities and quantities comprising man, we may note that they can be divided into *common* and *unique parts.* Common is that which is shared by all, although man may be dissimilar or unequal in quality or amount. For example, size is common to all, but height and weight vary; power is common to all, as is race. Moreover, there are also unique qualities and quantities, such as a person's face, his voice, his likes and dislikes, his loves and hates, and his body measurements. By heredity, environment, experience, and individual will, each of us is a unique event in nature; but by heredity, environment, learning, society, and culture, each person is an example of man, of a culture, of a society, of an occupation, of a family. We are thus a composite: in confirming our commonness, in reflecting our individuality.

But as social scientists trying to understand social interaction and conflict, our concern is not with what is manifested only in one man, with unrecurring, unpatterned, unique man, but with the common parts of his qualities and quantities, with man in general. At this point there are two ways to arrive at a framework for defining differences and similarities, and both end at the same place. In one we consider the common aspects of qualities and quantities, their variation, their patterns, and their constituent latent functions. This is the approach I took in *The Dynamic Psychological Field,* especially Chapters 10, 13, and 33, and I have taken it here, as well. But now my explicit concern is with the differences between two people. So let me choose the other route, which focuses on these distances.

We must find a way of discriminating between essence and accident, between the common and unique aspects of men. First, regardless of whether quality or quantity is essence or accident, let us compare the differences among all people on this dimension. I use the term *comparison* as a free variable ranging across binary and ordinal similarity and dissimilarity, and quantitative equality and inequalities. Thus two people will have an infinite variety of comparisons across all the qualities and quantities that could possibly characterize them.

Second, let us consider how these comparisons themselves vary across people. We will find that some comparisons are highly correlated, forming a pattern, a cluster. For example, there will be a pattern of differences associated with income, since people who differ in income usually differ in a variety of other characteristics, such as neighborhood, home, education, dress, and occupation. Similar examples could be given for those sharing the same religion, race, family, and so on. Thus the variation of people across a multitude of comparisons falls into patterns—intercorrelated clusters of comparisons.

Third, these patterns of comparisons define the common

aspects or parts of man. To see this, consider a unique aspect involved in a comparison. If a quality or quantity is truly unique, comparisons involving it will have no correlation with other comparisons. For example, if one man has a dozen fingers and all others have ten, every comparison between this person and all others involving number of fingers will produce a constant inequality of two; this comparison will stand by itself. That is, as we consider the variation among all comparisons involving all qualities and quantities, whether essence or accident, we will find that those involving man's unique aspects remain unique.

We have in this a general epistemological route to defining commonness, the same route that Hume took in defining inductively cause and effect and natural law. Commonness is given us by the *covariance* of the comparisons between men. Those comparisons based on common aspects in man's qualities or quantities will covary into empirical patterns. It is thus that we discern man and woman, father and child, rich and poor, powerful and weak. And it is thus that we can compare societies, as was done in *The Conflict Helix* (Part IX).

But these relationships between comparisons, these covariances, are are actually latent functions (Rummel, 1976, Section 10.2). They are the invariant *common* latents underlying all the manifest variation in the comparisons. And these common latent functions must be the *components* of a space of all the common aspects of qualities and quantities involved in these comparisons.

Before focusing on this space, let me review the logic. Man has qualities and quantities that are partially shared with others and partially unique. We can hypothesize comparing man —considering his similarities and dissimilarities, equalities and inequalities—on all conceivable qualities and quantities, and then determine the covariance among all these comparisons. The common aspects of the comparisons will form patterns of regularity, while the unique comparisons will remain unrelated to any other. Now, these patterns, being common latent functions, thus define the components of a common space of comparisons. It is a space comprising not only quantitative comparisons, *but binary and ordinal qualitative comparisons as well.* [13]

But what have I bought? Of what use is this space? Remember that my ultimate concern is to have a basis for saying that two people are alike or different; and related to this, to determine what is essence and what is accident. I have shown that covariance is a route to defining essence; that the covariances among the multifold variety of comparisons between people are reducible to a common space. This space has the following value.

People are located in this space on the basis of their many common similarities and dissimilarities and equalities and inequalities. That is, their locations represent their mutual likeness on their essential characteristics, attributes, and properties. We have not only a solution to defining essence, but also to determining how and in what way people are alike or different.

The proximity of people in the space then defines their likeness. And since this is a metric space, we can use now a more precise measure of likeness, or of similarity-dissimilarity, equality-inequality—namely, the *distance vector*. This vector between any two people being compared represents the overall difference between them; and the orientation of this vector, its direction, defines the components of this difference.

For example, consider the hypothetical comparison space of Figure 6.1, spanned by two components, wealth and power. These constitute two patterns of covariance underlying the diverse status comparisons among people (Rummel, 1976, Chapter 17). Within this space, as shown, individuals are distributed according to their closeness or likeness on these comparisons; and two such persons, i and j, appear in the first quadrant along with the distance vector from j to i. Note the various clusters of persons. These indicate or define those *species* or groups of people fairly close to each other on these comparisons relative to others: these clusters define types.

Henceforth, I use the term "distance" for the common similarity and dissimilarity, equality and inequality between two people in their essential characteristics, properties, or attributes. Distance stands for the magnitude of the distance vector in the comparison space just defined.

How do we know two people are alike? We assess the

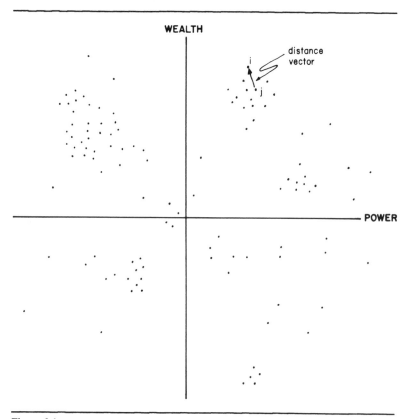

Figure 6.1

distance vectors between them.[14] How do we know in which way they are alike? We assess the components of their distance vectors. How do we know how people group in their distances from each other? We determine empirically what clusters exist in this space, as was done for state-societies in *The Conflict Helix* (Section 34.3). But here my interest is not empirical; rather, I want to assess theoretically likeness in its relation to solidarity or antagonism. So far, I have pushed the question up through layers of distinctions into common space. What remains to be assessed is the nature of the components of this space.

The common space, of course, is precisely the same as the sociocultural space (Rummel, 1976, Chapter 13) and the conflict space (Rummel, 1976, Section 28.1) latent in the conflict helix. For whether we begin with man as a field of expression defined by underlying latent functions as in *The Conflict Helix,* or with comparisons between characteristics, properties, and attributes, as here, we finish with the same common space. These are two routes to the same point of view. Thus the distance vectors between men in their sociocultural space are the *same* distance vectors entailed in comparing people.[15]

Since the common space is man's sociocultural space, the components are the same. These are the cultural components of language, religion-philosophy, ethics-law, science, and fine arts, and the social components of wealth, power, prestige, and class. The distances between people in the common space of all these components describe their likeness; the distances on these separate components, such as science or wealth, describe in which way two people are similar or different.

We now can deal more precisely with Sorokin's analysis of solidarity in the context of the conflict helix. First, however, I want to underline the ontology adopted here: what is similar or different is a point of view, a perspective on reality. Some emphasize the similarity of things, the genus, and strive toward defining the highest unity; some emphasize differences and analyze things into species and subspecies. Some see certain similarities as important, but others focus on different ones. All these perspectives are different actualizations of the potentials and dispositions existing in reality. In the light of our interests, of our problems, of our intentions, we confront the reality of other men with a framework of unity or differences; other men confront us with their power to manifest a specific reality. The balance between our perspective on unity and differences and the power of this reality constitute our perception.

For example, the particular component distances between people in sociocultural space will shift as we rotate its components. Yet nothing in the empirical comparisons between men will uniquely specify a rotation for this space. Consequently, an infinitude of perspectives on likeness all can be compatible with the same manifest comparisons. Of course the space is invariant and the distance across the whole space is invariant of rotations: only one space and overall distance are consistent with the same data. But even on this we get an invariant space and overall distance only if we assume the space to be Euclidean.

Given, then, that our view of likeness or difference is partially a perspective with which we confront nature, a perspective that is a condition of nature's intelligibility, how do we as social scientists investigating social interaction select an appropriate perspective? We do so in terms of a number of criteria, such as the moral implications, the comprehensiveness, the power of a perspective to make social reality intelligible, and simplicity. Above all, however, we select that perspective which helps us resolve our problems and answer our questions. In terms of my interest here, we select that perspective which best explains social interaction, such as solidarity and antagonism. The justification of the perspective I am adopting does not lie in the perspective (the space, distances, components) itself, therefore, but in its utility in helping us to understand interaction.

6.4 CONCORDANCE IN NORMS

In previous sections I presented Sorokin's analysis of the relationship of similarity and difference to solidarity and antagonism. His solution was to attempt throughout to subjectify differences, to treat them as a matter of individual meanings, values, and norms. With this conclusion in mind, I tried to provide a useful perspective for understanding similarity and difference, especially in relation to norms and values. The final questions now concern the precise meaning of norms and values in the light of man's common sociocultural space, and the relationship of the whole question of individual similarities and differences to the conflict helix.

What is a norm? In general it is a standard or role that guides or regulates behavior. Is there some other meaning, however, that is intrinsic to sociological analysis? When we consider what Sorokin (1969, Chapter 42) means, we find that norms define our highest moral standards, such as the Ten Commandments, or our most practical rules, such as those of etiquette, methodology, or good gardening (p. 47). This statement is clearly too broad for our purposes, since to say that interaction is dependent on similarities and differences in norms hardly focuses our comprehension well. We are then forced to ask about the kind of norms involved.

Perhaps others may provide a more useful meaning to norms. The *Dictionary of Sociology and Related Sciences* (1970) defines a norm as any "socially sanctioned mode or condition of behavior." This definition is even less helpful than Sorokin's. Three other definitions give some assistance. For Merton, norms are regulations about what are acceptable ways of achieving goals.[16] For Peter Blau (1967, especially p. 255), norms are standards of permissible conduct; and for George Homans (1961:46), a norm is "a statement made by a number of members of a group, not necessarily all of them, that the members ought to behave in a certain way in certain circumstances." Here we have norms as behavioral oughts, as regulators of interaction. They are our social ethics. I believe that norms as understood in this way fit precisely with Sorokin's conclusion about the relation of norms to solidarity and antagonism.

But, is not a norm also our expectation? Do we not expect others to behave according to our norms? In *The Conflict Helix* I defined our expectations (Chapter 3, Section 14.3) as the anticipated outcome of our behavior. We behave toward another person in the expectation that certain behavior or responses will result. This expectation has two aspects. First, there is an empirical ingredient, a learned expectation of another gained from prior interaction with him. A man may have learned, for example, that his wife becomes irritated if he burps at mealtime, his boss responds well to compliments, or his son balks at demands.

Clearly this aspect of expectations may not be normative. No ought or standard may be involved in our expectations as a learned outcome. The other may consistently act contrary to our norms or those of society, and with resignation, or with simply a wish to get along, we come to expect and accept this.

However there is one more ingredient, namely, our culturally learned expectations of another's behavior. We expect another to follow certain etiquette in responding to us, to obey certain implicit rules of the game, to act according to a certain morality. Society and culture are crosscut by these norms, which regulate behavior, and our expectations manifest them. For based on minimal information about another, we initially expect him to act as norms dictate. Only as we gain experience, do our expectations become more personalized and encompass deviation from cultural norms.

We can define two kinds of expectation, therefore, which combine to form our expected outcomes. Our *social expectations* are the outcome we expect according to our sociocultural and group norms. The norms serve as our generalized prediction of the responses of others; they provide us with an ability to swim through a sea of strangers. Our *personal expectations* comprise what experience leads us to anticipate about the response to our behavior from a particular other (such as a specific student named John) or a similar class of others (all students).

Social norms and social expectations thus are linked. Norms define the proper behavior in a society; our belief that people will so behave are our social expectations. Then the similarities or differences between two people in their social expectations of each other really reflect, to use Sorokin's terms, their concordance in norms.

And consider. Is not the structure of expectations and its congruence with an underlying balance of powers the measure of distance in expectations between individuals? Clearly it is. For it is through conflict that different expectations are corrected. And it is the structure of expectations that forms a congruence of expectations sufficient for cooperative—solidary—interactions.

6.5 SIMILARITY AND OPPOSITION IN VALUES

Mythology, religion and philosophy . . . are alike in that each has as its function the interpretation of experience in terms which have human value.

Joseph Wood Krutch,
The Modern Temper, Vol. I

Those studying social interaction, and especially conflict, have long recognized the importance of similarities or differences in values to harmonious or hostile relations. But here also we must ask, What are values? Sorokin is of no help, because he treats values as an implicit aspect of meanings and norms. Nor are other sociologists, for there is considerable confusion about values across the literature. Clearly a basic philosophical analysis is required. This may help in our understanding of values and in developing a conceptual framework consistent with our perspective on social interaction and the conflict helix.

When we say that Bob is good, the food is tasty, the government is bad, the kitten is cute, and the idea stinks, we are expressing values. The things named are being weighed by us; as concepts they are *evaluated* Adjectives like good, bad, and ugly express our feelings, our positive or negative sentiments toward things. To say something is bad (or terrible or horrible or outrageous) is to express negative affect, an emotional repulsion; to assert goodness of some sort, however, is to indicate that an attraction exists. We need not rely on intuition alone, however.

On the empirical level, analyses of concepts have shown consistently and cross-culturally that such an *evaluation* dimension is one of the kinds of conceptual meaning with which we endow things.[17]

One meaning of value is our *emotive* feeling toward things. Values, in part, refer to our disposition to endow that which we perceive with meanings like ugly or beautiful. But are not all values emotive? When we say that it is wrong to kill or lie and right to help others and turn the other cheek, are we not saying that these behaviors are good or bad, that they attract or repulse us?

Such is the ethical theory of many positivists, like A. J. Ayer (1946), who believe that all morality is reducible to emotive statements. I will not become involved in this popular argument here, reserving that fun for another book. However I can at least establish a line of attack incorporating another meaning of values—that involving ethics—which should enable me to clarify the relationship of values to interaction.

Although the matter is not undisputed,[18] the philosophical consensus is that Hume guillotined propositions about reality into two types:

In every system of morality which I have hitherto met with, I have always remark'd that the author proceeds for some time in the ordinary way of reasoning, and establishes the being of a God, or makes observations concerning human affairs; when of a sudden I am surpriz'd to find, that instead of the usual copulations of propositions, *is,* and *is not,* I meet with no proposition that is not connected with an *ought,* or an *ought not.* This change is imperceptible; but is, however, of the last consequence. For as this *ought* or *ought not,* expresses some new relation or affirmation, 'tis necessary that it should be observ'd and explain'd; and at the same time that a reason should be given, for what seems altogether inconceivable, how this new relation can be a deduction from others, which are entirely different from it.[19]

That is, statements about reality are of two logically distinct kinds. Those that describe or state what *is,* and those that state what *ought* to be. One cannot logically move from statements aobut what is to statements about what should be.

Statements about what should or ought to be comprise, however, our ethics, our morality. People should not kill; husbands should be faithful; children should be educated. But by Hume's analysis and contemporary philosophical opinion, such statements are logically distinguishable from beliefs about reality. Similarly, in Kant's analysis, reality as phenomena are what we experience—the realm of cause and effect, of natural laws. The realm of morality, of ethics, is nonempirical. It is the arena of pure reason, the domain of practical judgment.

We can therefore define a realm of values—our oughts, our morals, our ethics. Values of these kinds are of three types. First, our sociocultural *norms* or standards are the oughts that govern and regulate our social interaction, as already discussed. Second, *instrumental values* are the oughts that define the means, ways, routes, methods, structures, and so on for achieving some fundamental value. Thus democracy may be an instrumental value for achieving freedom, or the Good; welfare, for alleviating hardship; war, for protecting national values. Finally, the *fundamental* values, the ends, are usually non-negotiable and categorical. These are the basic oughts for which one is willing to sacrifice even himself. God, truth, freedom, equality, humanity, law, family, country have historically been the foci of such imperatives. They are our most basic ethics.

If values are emotive, instrumental, or fundamental, how do we know whether people are alike or different in their values? To begin with, such values are subjective. Each person will rate them in his own way, as a part of his psychological field.

Sociocultural norms can be identified with expectations. Is there such a one-to-one translation for values? First, I must determine what aspects, structures, or processes of the psychological field correspond to these values. Obviously important is the cultural matrix, which endows stimuli with meaning, values, and norms in the act of perception; it gives the initial weighting to reality. We do not see just a complex of lines, colors, and shapes, nor just a painting. We see a beautiful or ugly painting. We apprehend the world evaluatively. The cultural matrix defines our emotive values.

This creates a problem. For "differences or similarities between people in their cultural matrices" carries no empirical meaning. Certainly the cultural matrix underlies our perspectives, but "a perspectival distance" is too broad a term, since perspectives include personality and station, as well as the cultural matrix.

There is a solution, however, as indicated in the previous sections. If any psychological structure is suffused with emotive values, it is the attitudinal lattice that connects our basic needs with our day-to-day dispositions. Reflecting our emotive values are our attitudes toward abortion or a politician; our desire for a particular car or a higher salary; and our goals of helping the disadvantaged or learning to play the piano. Indeed, our positive and negative interests, which are simply our attitudes and their power to become manifest, are saturated with evaluation. To want very much to eat a steak, to buy a painting by Degas, to have the public water supply fluoridated, and to avoid inflation is to manifest attraction or repulsion with respect to such goals. And what else are emotive values?

For these values, then, the means of considering similarity and differences is clear: it is the distance vector between individuals in their cultural space. The components of this vector reflect fundamental differences in religion, science, ethics, and so on. But attitudinal differences also lie along this vector, for the larger the distance between individuals in cultural space, the more likely that their emotive attitudes are different, and the closer in this common space, the more likely they are to share the same attitudes.

Interests are activated attitudes. Therefore if the attitudinal differences and similarities lie along the distance vectors, this will also be true of interests. *Distances in cultural space reflect distances in interests.* And since interests are the basic motivational unit, the visible surface of our needs, sentiments, and roles, distances in interests also measure distances in needs like security, sentiments like self-esteem, and role attitudes.

This leaves us still with instrumental and fundamental values, with comparing the value hierarchies of individuals. The fundamental values are a person's ultimate regulating principles. Are these also reflected in interests? Of course. The ends and means of one's interests are surely regulated by moral judgment, and their content manifests his beliefs about killing, stealing, honor, loyalty, freedom, equality, and so on for however the Good is defined.

Here, however, we can be more specific about the nature of these interests than in the case of emotive values. Distinct interests (i.e., attitudes and their power to manifest behavior) coalesce as they share a common orientation toward man, society, and nature. Our interests combine as they reflect, say, a faith in the scientific method and empirical truth, a belief in the Buddhist creed, an appreciation and love of Japanese landscape painting. There is one pattern, however, one interrelated configuration of interests that consists entirely of values. These are attitudes toward the law's content and basic questions of moral personal and public policies. Should prostitution or the sale of pornographic materials be legal? Should there be capital punishment? Should there be amnesty for war deserters? Such are the stuff of politics and law, but our views on them, our attitudes that "I want the President's authority to make war taken away" or "I want to fight for Israel against the Arabs," are dispositions directly growing out of our fundamental values.

One component of intentional space involves these interests: the ethics-law component of our cultural subspace. Our location on this component—whether our ethics-law is hedonistic, transitory, relativistic, and totally sensory or a rational set of inflexible, God-given ideals—defines our fundamental values. Therefore to compare two people in their basic values, to assess their similarity or dissimilarity in ultimate oughts, is to consider their distance on the ethics-law component of cultural space.

Finally, there are the instrumental values that guide us in the achievement or maintenance of our fundamental values. Clearly, instrumental values as technical norms regulating the safe operation of a car (one ought to fasten his seat belt), doing scientific research (one ought to follow the scientific method to discover truth), or administering welfare are reflected in our varied interests. For all associated attitudes have an in-order-to aspect. I want to watch TV in order to relax or laugh or be entertained; I want to have public rapid transit in order to alleviate traffic congestion; I want to see an atmosphere of detente with the Soviet Union in order to lessen the risk of nuclear war.

But most attitudes involve instrumental values that as technical norms are relatively unimportant in comparing people, except perhaps methodologists (who may become quite emotional over whether one should use, say, factor analysis, causal analysis, or multidimensional scaling). There are, however, instrumental values that are fundamental values in their own right as well. Although socialism may be considered to be a means to mankind's greater happiness, it itself may become a pseudo-ultimate value; although democracy may be considered to be a means to preserving liberty, it can become another pseudo-ultimate. And so on for such instrumental values as public education, government regulation of business, or a minimum wage; churches, universities, or courts; communism, liberalism, or anarchism.

From this it should be clear that like our ultimates, instrumental values fundamentally mirror our statuses and our class membership—our social relationships. Our fundamental values are cultural in origin, but our means to satisfy them become our society, our division of labor. And the major cleavages in this society, which are between rich and poor, powerful and weak, honored and ignored, and especially, rulers and ruled, determine rewards. Most within the same culture share a desire for the same kind of rewards and benefits, but who gets how much, and when, are matters of class, of authoritative instrumentalities. Therefore instrumental attitudes are reflected in the distance vectors between individuals in their common social space. And again, people's interests lie along these distances.

The political formulas that move people are basically an amalgam of fundamental and instrumental values, of culture and society, of ethics, of status. And of class. Politics and political issues lie at the center of societies and their cultures. These are questions of power, authority and class, wealth and prestige. Who will lead? How will the leader or leaders be selected? What laws should be passed? How will privileges and sanctions be distributed? More concisely, who gets what, how, and when? Whether we are talking about the politics of universities, businesses, unions, cities, or states, or international relations, as they engage our interests, they fundamentally engage our basic ethics. *Our ethics—our fundamental oughts— endow our political interests with direction and strength.* To know that a person is a communist, a libertarian, a Nazi, a Roosevelt liberal, a Maoist is to have bracketed his fundamental ethical-legal values.[20] Political distances reflect such under- lying similarities and differences as political types correspond to different societies and cultures (Rummel, 1976, Section 34.2).

6.6 AND THE CONFLICT HELIX

We can now return to Sorokin's analysis of similarity and dissimilarity and his fundamental conclusion that the antago- nism between individuals depends on the basic similarity in their main values and the concordance in their norms. First, Sorokin's assumption that the important differences and simi- larities are in meanings, values, and norms, and not in objective characteristics, is an assumption of the conflict helix. For the space from which conflict stems is the *common* sociocultural space of meanings, values, norms, statuses, and class. The differences significant to social conflict define social relation- ships. And such are determined by the relative locations of individuals in their common sociocultural space, that is, their conflict space.

Second, the significant similarities and differences are measured by the distance vectors between individuals on the common components of the sociocultural space. These are the distances in religion, in science, in ethics, and so on for the cultural components, and in statuses and class for the social components. These distance vectors in sociocultural space define likes and unlikes, same and other, similarity and dissimilarity.

Third, attitudes, thus interests, lie along the distance vectors between individuals in their common sociocultural space. The different locations of individuals in this space reflect different interests; and the further apart the more likely it is that their interests will be opposed. In terms of the conflict helix, distances in sociocultural space and mutual awareness of them define the structure of conflict. The transformation of attitudes into interests creates the situation of conflict.

Fourth, the concordance of norms between individuals in interaction is a function of their structure of expectations. It is a function of the congruence between this structure and the underlying balance of interests, capabilities, and credibilities.

Fifth, according to Sorokin, antagonism is generated by the "opposite and diverse character" of the important values and norms and "in which the parties have no common system of values and norms." From the previous analysis, we can now rephrase this as follows. *Antagonism will be generated between men as they are distant in their expectations and interests.* Expectations define general norms, and interests cover the emotive, instrumental, and fundamental values. Also, the degree to which two people have a common system of values and norms is actualized in their interests, their balance of power, and their structure of expectations. With no common interests and social expectations, there can be no common system of values and norms.

Finally, the antagonism between individuals as a function of their expectations and interests, similarities and differences, depends on the conflict process. It depends on their mutual location in sociocultural space, on their awareness of the distances involved, on the activation of their interests, on their capabilities and credibilities, and on their balancing (which establishes concordant norms, a congruent structure of expectations).

In sum, Sorokin's conclusions are embodied in the conflict helix. The virtue of the helix is that it provides a clear definition of similarity and difference, taking into account qualitative and quantitative differences and imbedding these differences in an overall process of conflict that includes also culture, status, class, needs, attitudes, dispositions, interests, perception, power, and expectations. Thus the functioning of similarities and differences between individuals is understood as part of a sociocultural field. Differences alone do not create antagonism. But they are necessary ingredients in the antagonistic process, in the conflict helix.

NOTES

1. Plato, *Lysis,* 214.

2. Nicomachaen Ethics, Book VIII.

3. *Summa Theologica,* Part I of Second Part, O. 27, Art. 3.

4. See, for example, the empirical references mentioned in Davis (1966), Heider (1958), Burgess and Wallin (1943), Sorokin (1969, Chapter 7), and Berelson and Steiner (1964:305-309, 313).

5. Sorokin's categorization might resemble the stock market analyst's prediction, "The market will go up or down, or it could remain the same." Rather than developing a logical classification, Sorokin is inductively organizing the thinking of sociologists. To be logically complete, one also should pose the theory that both similarity and dissimilarity are independent of solidarity (or antagonism). No major thinker or scientist has proposed this, however; although by implication Plato came close to it through Socrates' inability to uncover the basis of friendship.

6. Mechanical solidarity is that of primitive or traditional societies based on similarity; organic is that of modern industrial societies characterized by extensive division of labor, which are sewn together by these differences. See *The Division of Labor in Society* (Durkheim, 1933).

7. Tönnies lumps all kinds of different elements into these two distinctions, which makes it difficult to distinguish them. In essence, however, it seems that gemeinschaft is a pattern of interaction involving fellowship, community, and love, whereas gesellschaft includes contractual and utilitarian types of interaction. Traditional sacred societies would be characterized by gemeinschaft; industrial secular societies by gesellschaft. See his *Gemeinschaft and Gesellschaft.*

8. For example, although men and women may use the same words, their modes of expressing these words through sentence structure, emphasis, and gesticulation are quite distinct.

9. In spite of their central role, values and norms as concepts are not subjected to any thoroughgoing analysis by Sorokin. He treats them as primitive terms. At the general macrolevel comfortable to Sorokin, this is consistent with his conclusions.

The problem comes in subjecting a generalization involving values to a microanalysis, for then the apparently clear meaning of the generalization evaporates. This is because an analytic treatment of values or ethics would reveal a profusion of independent distinctions. For example, value can refer to our disposition or sentiment toward something (whether we like it), an instrumental norm (we value money for what it can buy), or a basic end (the Good).

10. This would distinguish the so-called interval and ratio scales of measurement.

11. It is a common contemporary position to argue that things have no essence, but only relationships. Therefore, what a thing is depends on the relationships of concern to us. I disagree. To say that a thing is defined by its relationships is to imply *some thing* that exists apart from the relationship. My argument on this is in Chapter 34 of *The Dynamic Psychological Field* (1975).

12. In the context of a concern with same and other, similarity and difference, see, for example, Aristotle, *Categories,* 19-35.

13. Some mathematically oriented readers may question this. But we can denote binary qualities as zero or unity, and then the comparison between two people on this yields a difference of either zero (if they are similar) or plus or minus unity (if they are dissimilar); we can scale ordinal qualities and then compare two people by taking the ordinal difference. Consider next a matrix whose columns define the various qualitative-quantitative comparisons being made (as in religion, nationality, age, income, and education) and whose rows refer to specific pairs, such as John and Mary, Bill and Jean. Finally, consider a symmetric matrix comprising all the covariances (correlations) among these qualitative and quantitative comparisons. Then the eigenvectors of this matrix will approximate the latent functions of which I speak, and the eigenvectors in their totality will span the common space. Mathematically this will be a Euclidean space defining qualitative and quantitative comparisons.

14. The logic used here, the defining of a common space and distances between people in this space, underlies also a variety of approaches to similarities and differences being taken across the sciences. For example, pattern-search techniques being developed in mathematics, communications, and physics use similar approaches. See, for example, Watanabe (1969). Moreover, quantitative taxonomists in biology, trying to overcome the difficulties of the intuitive, genus-species approach, are employing the same approach to assess likeness that I am using. Foremost among them are Sokal and Sneath (1963), who recommend and elaborate methods identical to those I use in *Dimensions of Nations* (1972).

Multidimensional scaling and factor analysis are also similar logics for comparing individuals (Rummel, 1970, Chapter 22, on "Distance").

15. Specifically, one can begin empirically with attributes of individuals and define mathematically a space and its dimensions, the location of individuals within it, then their mutual distances. Or, one can begin with their differences and similarities on the attributes and mathematically define the space containing them as distances. In both cases the resulting space and distances are similar (see Rummel, 1970, Chapter 22).

16. See Merton (1957), particularly page 133, in reference to institutionalized norms.

17. See Osgood et al. (1957) and Miron and Osgood (1966). Besides the evaluative, two major dimensions of conceptual meaning are *potency* and *activity.*

18. See, for example, Hudson (1969).

19. *Treatise,* L. A. Selby-Bigge's edition, p. 469.

20. Of course those sharing the same political ideology may differ with respect to their honesty and their willingness to use unethical and immoral means to achieve their political goals. I am assuming that such differences are reflected somewhat by political interests, but mainly by the nonpolitical interests representing the emotive and instrumental values of a person.

Chapter 7

OTHER SOCIOCULTURAL CAUSES
AND CONDITIONS

I would . . . argue that it is useful to look at our own national life in these terms. If we examine the smaller groups which make up our vast and complex society, it is easy to see that divisions of interest and loyalties within any one group prevent it from standing in absolute opposition to other groups and to the society at large.

Gluckman, 1955:23-24

This chapter examines a few additional sociocultural hypotheses about the basis or causes of social conflict. My purpose is not to provide a comprehensive examination of the literature dealing with them, but to characterize each hypothesis and show its relationship to the conflict helix. The hypotheses concern cross-pressures, population, anomie, and acculturation.

7.1 CROSS-PRESSURES

A favored hypothesis that emerges in many guises is that man can be cross-pressured by his varied interests.[1] The interests may be contrasting or even antagonistic, as when I want to work on this book and go to the beach. They may be latent in unbalanced statuses (low wealth and high power), in contradictory roles (a superordinate in one group and a subordinate in another), in multiple group memberships (being a Catholic, a physicist, and a Republican), in multiple relationships (friends, family), or in personal dilemmas (being a husband and a homosexual). The essence of the cross-pressures notion is that interests pushing in opposite and diverse directions weaken our strength of purpose, undercut firm conviction or resolve, and facilitate compromise or concession.

This basically psychological view is carried to the level of societies by arguing that societies that enable a variety of conflicting and contrasting groups and interests to coexist drain off conflict through the fragmentation and segmentation of individual interests. Conflicts cannot polarize factions, oppositions do not become intense. Individuals do not become engaged in a battle over particular interests, simply because their social interests are segmented, confused, and contradictory.

On the other hand, if interests begin to coalesce into one societal cleavage, forming a conflict front that traverses society and divides groups and individuals into opposing clusters of homogeneous interests, conflict will be intense, violent, and possibly revolutionary.

This notion is central to my perspective. Where interests freely form and conflict, structures of expectations are based on mutual adjustments; there is a hubbub of continuous conflict in society as diverse and contradictory interests balance, work out differences, and establish a momentary modus vivendi for their coexistence. In the field of diversity lies conflict, but a unifying conflict. Cross-pressures operate at their maximum when field processes are given the widest scope. We then are buyers and sellers, workers and consumers, bureaucrats and citizens, superordinates and subordinates. We are dominant and subordinate; we win and lose.

But let antifields (coercive organizations) form, which weaken and eliminate cross-pressures, consistently placing the same people in the same dominant and subordinate relationships, and there is the making of class domination and eventual class struggle, dividing society. For interests will begin to polarize around support or opposition to the status quo. Interests previously fragmented, such as religion, career, party, and family, begin to divide along the we-they dichotomy. Such is the case in totalitarian societies, where all important social issues are a matter of state control and regulation, where all society is one clearly structured antifield, a coercive organization. All interests are a matter of supporting or opposing the status quo—the authoritative structure. Cross-pressures certainly exist within the segmented and isolated regions left to field processes, but at the societal level a totalitarian society is divided by antagonistic class interests whose intensity would destroy it—disrupt its one sovereign structure of expectations—if not held in check by countervailing coercion and force, by terror, mass execution, and pervasive concentration and "work" camps.

The fluidity of balances, the multiplicity of structures of expectations, the diversity and separation of antifields, attest to cross-pressures; the singularity of an antifield and the carving up of field processes within it shows the struggle of two interests: to rule versus to overcome.

7.2 OVERPOPULATION

A favored hypothesis is that conflict is a result of population pressure. Too many people make too many demands on each other and create intolerable frustrations, thus provoking social conflict. A solution is to halt population growth and better distribute existing populations. The attractiveness of this belief is a mystery, since history provides a profusion of counter-evidence. Violence, civil war and war, revolutions and pogroms all appear at one time or another among both densely and sparsely populated peoples. Nomads of the empty desert, horsemen of the wide steppes, traders on the limitless ocean have been involved in intense conflict no less than people in the most populous areas of the world. The most extreme acts of social violence—the extermination of whole populations, races, religions, or classes of cities and regions—cannot be localized by population density. Modern Russia and China, as well as ancient Greece, Gaul, Assyria, Persia, and Mongolia, Japan and the United States, Mexico and France, the British Isles and Italy—virtually no society in the broad sweep of history has escaped the most intense social cleavages and violence.

Surely, variation in population density cannot account for

this.[2] But without recourse to history, and on purely theoretical grounds, population density can have no consistent force. Population number is an objective, quantitative variable. Its importance in human affairs stems not from pure numbers alone, but from the meaning, values, and norms involved in the number of people. Crucial is the subjective significance of people, and this is a matter of culture and associated structures of expectations. As people grow in number, social needs and demands change. An increasing division of labor accommodates larger numbers, and multiple groups reflect and regulate their interests. All this is evolutionary, a matter of continual conflict, balancing, and a multiplicity of structures of expectations. But nothing inherent in the numbers argues for more, or less, intense or violent conflict. A city of ten million may have more, or less, intense conflict than a city of ten thousand. Societies like those in Belgium, the Netherlands, Japan, Taiwan, South Korea, or the United Kingdom may be theoretically more or less internally violent than societies like those in Laos, Venezuela, Argentina, Saudi Arabia, Canada, or Libya. What matters is whether the multiple expectations merge into one dominating antifield with a class structure of ins and outs. This defines the lines of intense struggle that can occur in sparsely settled or densely peopled territories.

The focus on population density as a cause of conflict is but a manifestation of an attitude prevalent in contemporary life. It is a belief in material, objective causes of human action, whether they be population, technology, poverty, climate, or urban blight. My argument is that such objective conditions are important insofar as they have meaning and values for men within their culture *and* individual perspectives. Moreover, even if important to man, such conditions are not causes of conflict but are particular aspects of their conflict structures, situations, balancing of powers, and structures of expectations. In short, their role is an empirical and not a theoretical matter. It involves a specific ase, not the general conflict process.

Man conflicts by virtue of opposing interests. No objectification of these interests is implied. Indeed, no objective conditions or facts may correspond to these interests. They may be wholly idealistic or imaginary as in conflicts over utopian features; wholly normative, as in conflicts over how society should be run; wholly authoritative, as in conflicts over the number of angels in heaven.

Even the most dangerous of social conflicts, that of classes, is of authority, of power. And this is a particularly psychological and social question of legitimacy and the normative order, of the *right* to command. There are no general objective conditions here. Class is a normative relationship, not a matter of objective wealth, poverty, resources, or the like. Even property, often considered to be objective or material, is a normative right. The social meaning of property is as a right of control and command, and major conflict is found to occur where this right has been called into question.

7.3 ANOMIE

Another hypothesis, developed to its fullest in the work of Durkheim (*Suicide,* 1951) and part of the contemporary consensual-equilibrium perspective on society, is that conflict results from a lack of normative integration into society. Criminals, delinquents, and radical groups have not been properly socialized or have lost their normative compass. Because of high family and personal mobility or rapid change in aspects of society, some individuals do not share the dominant norms, and they lack a sense of community, of belonging. Unguided by socially shared norms, they are uncertain and confused, prone to frustration and insecurity. Social conflict is then a manifestation of unintegrated individuals, of anomie.

There is much substance to this view, which on the sociocultural level provides understanding of the historical movement of revolution and war, as shown by Sorokin (1937-1941).[3] We commonly experience the problems of orienting outselves when immersed in a strange culture, either by traveling to another country or by participating in a different group. Without a knowledge of or sense for the prevailing meanings, values, and norms, we are uncertain, hesitant, insecure, and plagued with misunderstandings and misperceptions. We find it difficult to satisfy our interests, and this can lead to a feeling of opposition, of being put upon unjustly or irrationally. This feeling is heightened when we are members of groups or societies whose fundamental norms and values oppose our own, as a Protestant in a dominant Catholic culture, a leftist at a business convention, or a conservative in an American political science department. Normative isolation and loss of bearing is certainly a source of conflict.

How is anomie, then, related to the conflict helix? Under conditions of anomie, the relevant structure of expectations within which people interact is strained; it no longer represents a balance of interests, credibility, and capability. In anomie there is an incongruent structure of expectations, primed for a trigger provoking a balancing of powers and the creation of a new structure. Extensive crime and disorder, extensive disobedience and "immoral" behavior are signs that the societal consensus—the societal structure of expectations—is inadequate. It is doubtful whether incremental adjustments can save such a structure. Social breakdown and violence is the more likely mechanism for forcing norms and expectations into line with contending interests and their powers.

Through conflict, the individual is signaling dissatisfaction with existing rights and privileges. Through social conflict, he develops a working relationship with others and establishes his own rights. Through suicide or reflexive violence (an emotional lashing out), he expresses his powerlessness to alter the status quo.[4] Through conflict, dominating social groups are altered, and what was anomie at one moment becomes consensus with a new structure of expectations.

NOTES

1. For an excellent empirical analysis and overview of the literature, see Sperlich (1971).

2. Population density was included in many of the empirical studies described in *The Conflict Helix* (Rummel, 1976, Part IX) and generally was statistically independent of conflict manifestations. Empirical research provides no consistent basis for the belief that population pressure causes social conflict.

3. Sorokin's view is considered in more detail in Section 8.1.

4. See Rollo May (1972), who argues that powerlessness is the source of personal violence.

Chapter 8

AND PROCESS

> *The old order changeth, yielding*
> *place to new,*
> *And God fulfils himself in many ways,*
> *Lest one good custom should corrupt*
> *the world.*
>
> Tennyson, *The Passing of Arthur*

In my view conflict is a field process of interacting forces moving through time toward a balance of power—a momentary equilibrium, a curve on the helix. Although the particular helix form I give it is unusual, the idea of conflict as part of a social process is not. This chapter relates the conflict helix more explicitly to alternative process conceptions.

I treat process broadly as, alternatively, social change, cyclic movement, and stages of conflict. In the latter case, I deal with the theories of Sorokin, Marx, Johnson, and Richardson. The choices are not meant to be exhaustive, but exemplary. By linking the conflict helix and these theories, I hope to show that the helix in its different aspects integrates a variety of alternative views.

After considering these process theories, I turn to the social change and cyclic approaches.

8.1 SOROKIN ON CONFLICT

For Sorokin, extreme conflict is part of the process of rapidly changing social relationships. Sorokin saw social systems as causal-functional unities—as an integrated set of meanings, values, and norms; of social interaction; of official law-norms.

All societies change and the official law-norms of a group (such as a state) make provision for new law through legislatures, decrees, judicial interpretations, or constitutional revisions. These means of adjustment may not suffice, however, and a widening discrepancy between official law-norms and unofficial law convictions can develop. This can cause a growing and irreconcilable antagonism between two parts of the group, as one part supports official law and another feels that it is obsolete, unjust, exploitative, and so on.

The eventual consequence is a breakdown in organized relations—in the social equilibrium. The crystallized system of values and norms is disrupted; order and peace disappear. The result of this breakdown is conflict.

> Any organized intragroup or intergroup system of social relationships experiences change in the process of its existence.
>
> The change may be orderly, brought about by the constituted authorities of the group, according to its written or unwritten laws and constitution, or according to the desires and mores of its members.
>
> In other cases, the change proceeds along different paths. The organized network of relationships of a given group, or the system of intergroup relationships, breaks down, contrary to, and regardless of, the laws, constitution, mores, and authorities.
>
> When this crystallized system is broken, the organized group becomes disorganized, the organized relationships between the groups cease to be such. Order and peace (equilibrium) disappear either in the life of the group, or in the relationship between interacting groups.
>
> Such a confusion leads generally to a growth of conflicts between the members (in the group) and between interacting groups. Increase of conflict means coercive antagonism in its open form, in the form of sheer violence applied by one party to another. [Sorokin, 1957:535] [1]

With this perspective, Sorokin set out in the 1930s to determine the historical trends in war and internal disturbances. He developed a scale of the intensity, duration, scope, and importance of these conflicts, which he plotted over quarter-centuries for classical Greece, for Rome, and separately for the major European nations.[2] He found the following trends:

(1) No upward or downward periodicity or trend to war or internal disturbances exist—they just fluctuate through time.

(2) War and internal disturbances occur for all societies and cultures—sensate and ideational supercultural systems are neither more nor less peaceful or belligerent.

(3) War and internal disturbances show no positive or inverse association.[3]

(4) Wars and revolutions tend to increase during periods of transition from sensate to ideational culture and vice versa.

(5) The peak of internal disturbances are periods of transition in social relations—the historical turning points.

From this empirical-historical survey, Sorokin concludes that the cause of inter- and intragroup peace is a well-integrated system of values. The values must be in harmony and mutually compatible. The cause of war or internal disturbances is then a disruption of this integration, and any factors that contribute to the disintegration contribute to war and revolution.

The "main and the indispensable condition for an eruption of internal disturbance is that the social system or the cultural system or both shall be unsettled" (Sorokin, 1957:602, italics omitted).

Briefly, this is Sorokin's view of conflict.[4] First, conflict is a manifestation of rapid transition between different systems of organized relationships. As such, conflict and violence appear to be "permanently working forces, inherently connected with the essence of social life itself, which do not permit either a complete elimination or the unlimited growth of disturbances" (Sorokin, 1957:592).[5]

Second, manifest conflict is a resultant, an effect, of this breakdown, as are the sore throat and running nose of a sick person; these effects play no role in curing the disease that causes them. Third, Sorokin has no conception of latent conflict or conflict situations. Values or official and unofficial law-norms become incongruent, and disruption causes unrest and conflict. The idea of incipient or latent conflict groups or classes, of a situation or structure of conflict, is not an explicit part of his perspective, although implicit within it.

Fourth, he ignores the mechanism by which the disruption or breakdown occurs. The idea of trigger events is not mentioned in this context. There is simply incongruence and incompatibility of values; then disruption.

Finally, his view provides no role for power or power balance.[6] Somehow, disruption occurs and causes violence, and during the violence (say, in the constructive phase of a revolution) old social institutions that were washed away in blood are reconstructed much as they were before, but with new elite and new justification for them. Power, manifested through coercive violence, enters only during periods of transition. With no role during periods of crystallized values, conflict is abnormal—deviational. Thus the notion of conflict serving society is uncongenial to Sorokin. Harmony and compatibility in values and norms integrate society, not conflict.

How does Sorokin's view relate to the conflict helix? Clearly, much is reflected in the helix. The idea of conflict being most intense during a system transformation in values or norms, as well as the ideas of violence being caused by disruption, and of crystallized values and norms, are part of the helix perspective. Moreover, the helix is within a field of meanings, values, and norms, which is also the stuff of Sorokin's society. There are, however, the following differences.

First, the conflict within the helix has explicit latent phases. Sorokin articulated no such phases. He does not have a concept of the latent movement from conflict structure to manifestations, thus cannot explain how groups or individuals move from harmony and equilibrium to conflict.

Second, he has no coherent notion of status quo or class conflict, thus has no orienting concept for understanding the actual lines of conflict—the conflict front—in society.

Third, the helix conflict contains a mechanism for change, for balancing incompatible interests. Thus like a fever to a disease, conflict serves as both symptom and cure.

Fourth, the resulting equilibrium or structure of expectations is founded on a balance of power and can become incongruent not only as values or norms become incompatible, but as the power balance itself becomes increasingly unbalanced.

Fifth, the structure of expectations is not necessarily a consensus or agreement on values, or a compatibility. It may be based almost wholly on coercive power, as in slave labor camps or prisons.

Finally, random events or triggers initiate conflict once the situation is ripe or can disrupt an incongruent structure of expectations.

Sorokin's deep insight into the process of conflict and his historical documentation of this process was a great contribution to our knowledge. The conflict helix does not contradict his insights or evidence, and this construct should be seen as an elaboration and extension of his conclusions, as a completion of the spiral picture whose portions he saw so well.

8.2 MARX

In Section 5.1 I summarized Marx's class theory and described its relationship to my conception of class. Clearly, I accept class struggle as the engine of conflict and violence throughout a society, but I define class difference as between ruled and rulers. Classes ultimately form around the right of command, not private property, as for Marx.

I also outlined the process of class conflict as Marx saw it: the creation of three great classes based on property (land, capital, labor); the exploitation of labor power; the utilization of state power by capitalists to support this exploitation; the growing homogeneity of each class, as capitalists eliminate one another and gain in wealth and workers sink into extreme poverty; the generalization and organization of the class struggle; the absorption of the landowning class into the bourgeoisie, the growth of class consciousness and overt struggle; and the breakdown of capitalist society and success of the working class. The process begins with capitalist society and ends with its revolutionary transformation to a classless, proletarian society.

Within the helix, antagonistic classes exist in all societies. Moreover, there is no inevitable movement from the latent class structure to overt struggle and revolution. The resolution of class conflicts depends on crosscutting class memberships and the segmentation of interests and power. Moreover, within the helix revolution does not end class conflict; instead it leads to a new class configuration based on a balance of power between the new rulers and ruled. A new latent class conflict is thus created.

Moreover, if we understand class to be organized around the status quo supported by and reflected in authoritarian roles, we can apply the conflict helix to modern industrial societies, whether socialist or capitalist, and develop thereby a better understanding of the process of conflict between workers and managers, bureaucracies and citizens.

Then how does the conflict helix relate to the process of conflict spelled out by Marx? First, it reflects his insight into conflict as a generator of social, structural change. Second, it reflects his focus on class conflict as basic to this change at the societal level. Third, it reflects his belief in ideology, values, and norms as a mirror of class relationships (in the helix view, as a mirror of the balance of power). Fourth, it supports Marx's belief that power is a basic ingredient in the process, and conflict of power, a basic mechanism. Finally, it reflects his view that conflict structures exist underneath social phenomena, and to understand the process of manifest conflict requires beginning with the organization of latent conflicts in society.

8.3 CHALMERS JOHNSON

In *Revolutionary Change* (1966) Chalmers Johnson presents a dynamic theory of revolution[7] that marries the consensus-equilibrium perspective on society and the conflict or coercive view. He sees revolution as occurring within a social fabric, a social context.

Johnson views society as a system of roles and status-oriented behavior guided by norms. Roles, statuses, and norms are his major social elements, and values, his social medium. Values are behavioral expectations or social gestalts (1966:24), which coordinate the social system. They enable individuals to orient their behavior.

A harmonious society is an equilibrium between values and the division of labor (environment). There is a "synchronization" between values and the division of scarce resources and labor. However in all societies changes occur in both values and environment, such as through global communication, rise of external reference groups, intellectual innovations and new ideas, and technological developments, creating a constant need for adjustment between values and environment to maintain equilibrium.

All societies contain homeostatic devices for sustaining value equilibria, such as the control of deviancy, avoidance and routinization of conflict (e.g., collective bargaining laws), and legal sanctions. Moreover, there are ways of incrementally altering the structure of society—for example, through an accumulation of legislation (as under Roosevelt, 1932-1944) or a series of judicial reinterpretations of a constitution. These may be either unconscious adjustments without intent to change the system, or policies that deliberately alter the system to maintain or reinstate synchronization between values and environment, such as racial integration and affirmative action legislation in the 1960s and 1970s in the United States.

If homeostatic devices fail, a growing value-environment disequilibration creates a revolutionary situation. According to Johnson, the process of revolution is then the following:

- Change in values or environment or both creates a disequilibration between them.

- Homeostatic devices, including incremental adjustment and structural change policies, fail to reinstate synchronization; or the elite may resist making the required changes.

- *Power deflation* occurs, which means the elite must rely increasingly on force to maintain order.

- *Loss of authority* follows, which means that the elite's use of force is seen as illegitimate, and the threat of sanctions becomes the means of regulating society.

- Personal tensions are heightened.

- Latent interests associated with the superordinate-subordinate divisions in society polarize into manifest interest groups supporting or opposing the status quo.

- The development of a revolutionary ideology overcomes the conflict retarding effects of multiple role playing and polarizes society into two groups: one seeking to maintain the status quo, and one seeking to overthrow it.

The process just described leads to a situation ripe for revolution. There is a manifest cleavage in society between supporters and opponents of the status quo. This situation is characterized as follows:

- The final sufficient cause of revolution is a trigger event ("accelerator") that deprives the elite of force (e.g., mutiny by a military division) or proves to the revolutionaries that they stand a chance of success (e.g., a show of weakness by the elite, such as inability to stop a demonstration).

In sum, dissynchronization + power deflation + loss of authority + accelerator = revolution.

In relation to the conflict helix, several differences and similarities can be noted. First, Johnson's starting point is the value-coordinated society. He begins with order and asks why disorder (revolution) occurs. This is the wrong starting point, for it neglects the important matter of how the original order came into being. In the conflict helix, societies grow out of individual interests, conflict of interests, and balances of power. Order is then an arc of the spiral, the structure of expectations based on a congruence between interests (thus values and wants), capability, and credibility. Johnson begins with the congruent structure of expectations, without specifying its origin in conflicts of interests and its base as a balance of power.

Second, Johnson is perceptive in stating that increasing incongruence between values and environment creates a situation ripe for revolution, and his concepts of power deflation and loss of authority further our understanding. In the helix view, an established structure of expectations represents a value consensus in that the parties have worked out an implicit contract governing their interactions and the distribution of rights and privileges—that is, the status quo—which they are willing to live with. This structure, as in Johnson's theory, may become incongruent with changes in the underlying power balance as interests, power, or the perceived capability of one or another party are altered. Moreover, adjustments to this incongruence may be incremental or through policies that result in a change in the status quo (such as income redistribution tax laws). As the incongruence between expectations and power balance increases, however, so does the likelihood of a revolutionary outbreak.

Third, the dissynchronization between values and environment is accompanied by a consistent cleavage of society into those supporting and opposing the status quo. The members of these opposing groups come from subordinate versus superordinate statuses. In the helix also, societal conflict is manifested by such a polarization into opposing class interests, which is an aspect of the developing incongruence in expectations and power balance. Johnson, however, avoids defining classes and authoritarian role hierarchies. He defines opposing groups in terms of statuses, therefore losing the analytical and empirical strength of the Marx-Dahrendorf approach.

Fourth, as the incongruent structure of expectations is disrupted by a trigger, Johnson's dissynchronized and polarized society erupts into violence, catalyzed by certain events. Such events both in the helix and for Johnson work on man's will. They stimulate the decision to act, either by displaying the other's weakness or encouraging one's belief in success. Moreover, the trigger may be random, a chance happening.

Fifth, for Johnson the process ends with revolution. Thus he begins with order and ends with disorder. He does not deal with the order-creating function of revolution, its violent balancing of interests and power that eventuates in a new elite, a new status quo, and a new structure of expectations undergirded by a new balance of interests, capabilities, and credibility.

Sixth, Johnson develops a process view of revolution that could be generalized to all levels of conflict. The ideas of power deflation, loss of authority, dissynchronization of values with environment, and so on can apply to family conflict, university unrest, strikes, and international relations. Johnson implied this when he used his theory to explain the Berkeley student rebellion in 1964 (1966:xiii). But he does not make this explicit. The conflict helix is explicitly general. It is meant to explain the process of conflict at all levels. It is a view of man contra man, of order-disorder-order, no matter what the context.

Finally, Johnson views society as a system of elements and functions. His revolutionary process is part of the functioning of society and serves to bring about structural change. There are roles, statuses and norms, and values and the division of labor that are the interconnected parts of the social system. The notion of a field of forces—of a gestalt, a balance, a medium of values, meanings, and norms, a causal-functional unity—is inconsistent with Johnson's view. Like a watch, his *system* is a well-ordered organization of parts. Thus revolution occurs when these pieces are out of "synchronization." For the helix, however, societies are balances of forces, a momentary gestalt among a variety of pulling and pushing powers. They are fields and antifields, crosscutting conflicts and cleavages, latents and manifestations, potentialities and dispositions.

8.4 LEWIS FRY RICHARDSON

Among the many attempts to model social processes,[8] the most scientifically influential have been Richardson's arms race models (1960). The conflict process reflected in them has been called by Rapoport (1960) the Richardson processes.

Briefly, Richardson conceives of arms races as mutual aggravating processes, where the rate of change in the armaments of each party is dependent on the other's threat, plus one's own level of defense, the restraining cost of defense, and one's grievances. Whether an arms race ends in equilibrium, disarmament, or war depends on the mutual balance between threats, defenses, costs, and grievances.

In equation form, let x stand for the defense of nation i, and y the threat of nation j to i. Then, as a first approximation, the leaders of nation i will adjust their defenses to this threat such that

$$\frac{dx}{dt} = ky \qquad (8.1)$$

Similarly, the leaders of nation j will adjust their behavior to the threat of i such that

$$\frac{dy}{dt} = cx \qquad (8.2)$$

The equations say that the rate of change in the defenses of each party is a function of the threat of the other. The constants k and c then represent the fear and insecurity associated with this threat. The larger the fear, the greater the positive rate of change in one's defenses as a consequence of the other's threat.

This first approximation is not altogether satisfactory because the defined process is unstable: it must continuously escalate to war, unless neither side threatens the other (x = y = 0). A threat from either inevitably leads to war.

This is unrealistic, claims Richardson. Therefore, as a second approximation, assume that the cost of defense is a restraining influence, where cost should be understood in terms of alienating domestic support as well as budgetary cost. Then we can rewrite the equations as

$$\frac{dx}{dt} = ky - ax \qquad (8.3)$$

$$\frac{dy}{dt} = cx - by \qquad (8.4)$$

where a and b are coefficients representing the restraining influences of defense costs.

Yet these revised models are not complete. They say that war or stability is a consequence only of a threat-insecurity-defense-costs nexus—a pure threat and response system. But other elements must be involved. Surely, threat and response reflect desires and ideals that should be incorporated. To accommodate them, Richardson uses the constants g and h for the aggregate interests of each side. Then we have

$$\frac{dx}{dt} = ky - ax + g \qquad (8.5)$$

$$\frac{dy}{dt} = cx - by + h \qquad (8.6)$$

These are the final models. It should be recognized that *they are general social conflict process equations,* where the result can be war, revolution, violence, murder, divorce, or a fight. They describe any mutually aggravating process of social interaction. Most important for our purposes, they describe the formation and disruption of structures of expectation.

In this light and relating now Richardson's process equations to the conflict helix, let me draw out the implications of these models.

First, the models display a mutual balancing between threats (x, y), perception and resulting insecurity (k, c), defense costs (ax, by), interests (g, h), and behavior (dx/dt, dy/dt). That is, the conflict interaction between parties is a mutual balancing of threats, capabilities (costs), and credibility (i.e., insecurity). This is precisely the balancing of power in the conflict helix. Richardson's models particularize to arms races the general balancing of power phase of all conflict processes.

Second, Richardson's models also reflect the psychological field underlying the conflict process, the field of situation (perception), personality, expectations, and behavioral disposition. In his models, the situation is the threat (x, y) of the other; the personality is bound up in two sets of interests (motivations), which are those associated with defense costs (ax, by) and grievances (g, h) against the other party; the expectations are the credibility or, in his terms, insecurity (k, c) associated with the other's threat; and the behavioral disposition is the rate of change (dx/dt, dy/dt). My model for the conflict helix (Rummel, 1976, Chapter 33) and Richardson's models are mathematically different animals. The discrepancy reflects differences in ontology and epistemology, but it should not obscure the basic conceptual similarities in psychological and social perspectives.

Third, and moving more specifically to the formal implications of Richardson's models and treating them as general conflict process models, if g, h, x, and y are zero, there will be continuous peace. That is, if there are no mutual threats and no opposing interests, there will be no conflict, thus no violence or war. As for the conflict helix, a condition for the initiation of the conflict process is the creation of opposing interests (the conflict situation) or threats, which by their nature create opposing interests.

Fourth, if one party does not defend against the other's threat (thus x or y = 0, but not both) even though he has opposing interests (g and h are positive), in this case of "unilateral disarmament" the situation will not be stable. The other's threat will force one to increase defenses, which will in turn push the other's defenses (threat) to higher levels. The threat of one's capability in a situation of opposing interests leads to defensive reactions. For Richardson, turning the other cheek does not assure a stable relationship when one's interests oppose those of another. Similarly in the conflict helix, opposing interests are the necessary condition for the conflict to be manifest. In the helix view, however, one may elect not to defend, one may not manifest conflict. The other party may be too powerful and too credible. Submission may be the only route to protect some interests, if only personal survival. But Richardson does not make explicit provision for this.

Fifth, if both parties simultaneously eliminate their threats and defenses, the situation will continue to be unstable if opposing interests exist. This is because $dx/dt = g$ and $dy/dt = h$. Again, opposing interests are the key, as in the helix. A situation of conflict is bound to turn into a mutual threat-defense reaction system.

Sixth, if the defense and insecurity (cx, ky) terms predominate, the system will escalate to overt conflict (war, for Richardson). The same is true in the helix, where the intensity of threat (capability) and insecurity weight opposing interests. The greater this weight, the more likely a trigger will precipitate overt conflict.

Finally, by setting $dx/dt = dy/dt = 0$, a point of intersection between the lines representing equations [8.5] and [8.6] may be found. This would be a balance of power, an equilibrium point. It is where both sides feel that their insecurity, interests, defenses, and costs are balanced against the other's threats. The existence of such an equilibrium depends on the balance between these elements (i.e., that $a/k > d/b$ or $ab > kc$). This equilibrium is comparable to the structure of expectations in the helix; it is where interests, capabilities, and credibility balance. Moreover, for Richardson as in the helix, the balance can drift toward conflict as it becomes unstable because of underlying change in its supporting elements.

The Richardson process equations are very close to modeling the conflict helix. The rhetoric is different, and Richardson deals with only a portion of the process—conflict situation to conflict balancing or to equilibrium and disruption—and only in the context of arms races and war. Moreover, in the interest of scientific parsimony, Richardson ignores the many distinctions made in elaborating the conflict helix (triggers, congruence, structure of conflict, distances, etc.). Nonetheless, his models reflect remarkably well the process of social conflict.

8.5 CHANGE

One of the more popular explanations for the occurrence of conflict and violence is change. Change works to upset the social equilibrium, to alter roles and expectations, to transform values. It creates a cultural lag, a gap between the material conditions of society and the sociocultural complex of values and norms. It is difficult to untangle the precise meaning of change in such explanations and to determine what the independent change-as-cause may be. Without embedding it in some qualifying phrase, such as "change in material conditions," "change in available land," "change in property values," or "religious change," the idea of change producing conflict seems to be more a philosophic perspective than a sociological theory.

One way of qualifying change has been a strong motif in the literature: as *technological change.* Technology can be defined as the means of production, transport, communication, and violence (e.g., weapons); or industrial level, character of dwellings, and the development of writing, mathematics, and science. And in search of a commonality to all these elements, technology may be defined by the total energy available or that produced by such prime movers as the water wheel, the steam engine, and the gas turbine. However defined, the fundamental idea is that technological change creates the conditions for conflict.

The effect of technological change is usually discussed in one of two ways. First, such change can be seen as occurring more rapidly than society can adjust. This creates a maladjustment—a *cultural lag*—which leads to instability and conflict. Thus if changes in the environment make possible the realization of values not being satisfied by an existing cultural complex of norms and mores, attitudes, and institutions, this disparity is defined as cultural lag. The basic normative aspect of this idea is clear: cultural lag is the difference between what *is* and what some segments of society think *ought to be.* Technology creates the means for satisfying certain values, while existing norms, attitudes, or institutions inhibit or block such satisfaction.

The effect of technological change can also be considered through the notion of an equilibrium of values—the complex of desires and attitudes. Values are seen to eventually balance each other in society such that there is a general equilibrium between wants and costs, investments and rewards, capabilities and power. The balance of power systems among states are seen as such equilibria.

This equilibrium is based on certain realities, such as resources, abilities, physical barriers, and distance, which limit desires and attitudes. Realities may gradually change, however, and the value equilibrium can slowly adjust, as happens in a free market system.

Technology then affects the realities of value equilibria. Change in technology alters these realities, and if this change is too rapid, the equilibrium in values becomes increasingly unstable. Maladjustment becomes more severe, the balance is disrupted, and conflict occurs. Conflict then serves to establish a new equilibrium in line with changed realities.

The similarity between these ideas and the helix perspective can be clarified by reference to *The Conflict Helix* (Sections 32.2, 35.2). The theories that point to technological change as the villain are focusing on the causes of increasing incongruence in the structure of expectations. A balance of power is formed (in my terms) among interests, capabilities, and credibilities. This is a working arrangement, an implicit or explicit contract, enabling people to interact without conflict regarding their individual interests. It is an equilibrium of values, to be sure. But technological innovations, such as machine guns, the steam engine, the assembly line production of items made from interchangeable parts, and the telephone, alter the conditions of the balance. Capabilities are changed; interests are transformed or created; credibility is newly perceived. The *is, can,* and *oughts* become incongruent with this balance, and increasingly the status quo is unacceptable. Whether called cultural lag or disequilibrium in values, the fundamental idea is of incongruence, disruption, and conflict. Conflict then is the means through which is formed a new balance more in line with the technologically altered elements.

Technological change not only influences the balance underlying the structure of expectations, but also the creation of a structure and situation of conflict. Developments, such as the automobile, radio, movie, and television create new attitudes and transform the old. Thus where there is differential development, attitudes can be brought into opposition, such as between urban and rural regions or developed and undeveloped societies. Technology can also transform a structure of conflict into a conflict situation. By increasing contacts between different and opposing cultures and groups, it creates *awareness* of differences. Moreover, technology provides the means for extensive communication, propaganda, and organization, which can rapidly actualize class consciousness and marshal class antagonisms.

Clearly, technological change is a disturbing element in society. But it is unsettling only insofar as it brings attitudes into opposition, increases the awareness of this opposition, transforms these attitudes into opposing interests, and changes the balance underlying the structure of expectations.

Change has been interpreted as technological. Let me now broaden the idea of change to comprise any alteration, transformation, or modification of a social relationship or any new event, condition, or rule affecting that relationship. A new baby, a marriage, a job, or a law; fire, earthquake, or flood; hospitalization, injury, or death; maturation, graduation, or retirement: all are changes, and all affect social relations.

Change so conceived occurs constantly. Nonetheless, there are periods in human affairs when changes come fast and furious, as in times of revolution, war, depression or hyper-inflation, or natural disasters. And there are periods of quiescence and little change.

The conflict helix is the process of adjustment to all such change. New events require new adjustment. Although a structure of expectations can absorb change through incremental reinterpretation of rules and understandings, changes in behavior, and piecemeal accommodations, a rebalancing of power is necessitated by a rapid pace of change or by radically new events. All that is needed then is a trigger, a catalyst, for conflict to ensue.

8.6 CYCLES

The notion that conflict and violence are cyclic in human affairs is reflected in the literature on conflict. War and revolution are seen as periodic occurrences, and conflict as a swing in the pendulum of social life. Cycles exist in all kinds of natural phenomena; that they appear in human affairs is a reasonable hypothesis.

Through his principle of limits, Sorokin provides a good explanation of how cycles can occur in sociocultural systems. Sociocultural systems are divisible into two opposing types: sensate and ideational. Each flowers and develops its potential, which is then exhausted as the system moves to extremes. Opposing system elements accumulate until the system breaks down and is transformed into its opposite. Although Sorokin feels that his historical, empirical results show only fluctuation and not cyclic periodicity, his theory is fundamentally cyclic.

Is the conflict helix a cyclic theory? The balancing, balance, disruption, rebalancing phases of the helix indeed appear to be cyclic. For people or groups in continuous contact, the interactions they experience seem to move through cycles of conflict and equilibrium, of which the helix appears to be an excellent explanation.

But we are dealing with a *spiral,* not a periodic process. All other things constant, as people move through the conflict, balance, conflict, balance process, they are learning. Each balance is not *de nova* but is partially based on the experience of previous balances and conflicts. Thus if a marriage withstands the stresses of new children or in-laws moving in, or such crises as severe sickness or loss of job, it moves toward more stable and durable structures of expectations. In other words, the amplitude of the cycle decreases while the period increases in time.

To be sure, few interactions are isolated. Exogenous events constantly influence the balance underlying a structure of expectations. Inflation, unemployment, an invention, or the rise of an unusually gifted leader may disrupt a balance of power. Nonetheless, through experience people learn to adjust, their expectations stabilize, and they are less prone to conflict.

But generations die. And with them go personal structures of expectations. New ones come into being with new interests, new perspectives, and a need to balance anew. Surely new generations inherit the expectations of the older through culture and social institutions. However each generation must reinterpret these structures through its own perspectives, thus initiating new social processes and determining new balances through conflict.

It is thus that the life of an individual reflects a helix, but the long-term life of a social system may be more periodic.

This is pure conjecture, however, and we need more analyses of historical change to establish what generational cycles exist. At the manifest societal level some generations are blessed with periods of relative peace and harmony, while others are condemned to continuous troubles, strife, unrest, and violence. Beneath this surface, cyclic patterns may tie into the generational turn over and the initiation of societal conflict processes by newly mature individuals.[9] An historical birdseye view shows the fluctuation of sensate and ideational cultures, of peace and war, revolution and integration, democracy and tyranny, and, above all, the to and fro of the incessant class war between the ins and outs, the rich and poor. In this macro-, cross-generational view, the conflict process seems to be cyclic.

NOTES

1. See also Sorokin (1969:481-482).

2. The empirical evidence is given in Sorokin (1937-1941, Vol. III). It is abridged in Sorokin (1957, Chapters 32-35) and summarized and supplemented with additional corroboration in Sorokin (1969, Chapters 31-33).

3. This holds also for successful versus unsuccessful wars (Sorokin, 1957:597).

4. Sorokin also attributes murder and the fluctuation in severity of criminal punishment to the breakdown of social relations and transition periods (1969:513-514).

5. Sorokin is talking here about internal disturbances, but the essence of his overall conclusions leaves no doubt that this would apply to war as well.

6. Sorokin consistently ignores the dynamics of power. The active use of social power to achieve one's ends, the balancing of different interests through the assertion of power, the role of capability and credibility, and the support and implementation of social values and norms given by a particular configuration of powers between ruled and rulers, find little reflection in his work. He takes a consensual or equilibrium view of society. Consensus over values and norms develops, somehow, and unifies society.

7. Many of the elements of Johnson's theory can be seen in Gurr's (1970) model of violence and its underlying frustration-aggression assumption discussed in Section 33.2. Johnson assumes no such psychological basis and treats the root causes as sociological, as we see later.

8. See, for example, Simon (1957), Coleman (1964), and Rashevsky (1949).

9. From data that do not appear cyclic, one cannot assume that cycles are lacking. Underlying cycles, in their joint effects, can produce noncyclic movements and even a linear trend.

PART III

CONFLICT IN PHILOSOPHICAL PERSPECTIVE

There is something in this more than
natural, if philosophy could find it out.

Shakespeare, *Hamlet* II, ii

Chapter 9

OPPOSITION, DETERMINISM,
AND INEVITABILITY

> *The two extremes appear like man and wife,*
> *Coupled together for the sake of strife.*
>
> Charles Churchill, *The Rosciad*

9.1 THE CONFLICT OF OPPOSITES

As everybody knows, war and peace transform themselves into each other.

Mao Tse-tung, *Selected Works,* Vol. 2

For ages man has been captivated by a philosophy of opposition, a belief in reality as a manifestation of an underlying struggle between opposing or contradictory tendencies, elements, or forces. An insight into the nature of these oppositions was believed to provide as essential understanding of all things, and of harmony, strife, and change.

Greek philosophers, under the influence of Anaximander (Durant, 1939:138) and, especially, of Heraclitus (Burnet, 1957), believed that reality comprised opposites whose unity manifested all things. For Heraclitus, the "formula" for understanding reality was the perpetual strife of opposites. No simple empirical opposition, this was a connection between opposites such that one cannot exist or be perceived without the other, as with the day-night, up-down, hot-cold. "Men do not know what is at variance argues with itself. It is an attunement of opposite tensions, like that of the bow and the lyre"[1] and wisdom is to perceive this underlying opposition.

This philosophy is remarkably similar to the yin-yang of classical Chinese philosophy, elaborated in the commentaries of *I-Ching*. The yin and the yang are complementary principles or forces, explaining all processes of development and decay. Yin is the negative, passive, weak, or destructive element existing in all things, and yang the coexisting positive, active, strong, and constructive element. All change manifests an interaction between these forces; harmony is their equilibrium, conflict their opposition.

This philosophy can also be found in the Pair of Opposites of Buddhism (Humphreys, 1955), or in the blending of the two antagonistic forces (the life-monad versus matter) in non-Aryan Indian philosophy (Zimmer, 1969:379), in medieval Christianity (as in the *coincidentia oppositorum* of Nicholas of Cusa),[2] and in contemporary non-Marxist philosophies.[3]

A belief in a fundamental opposition in all things has had its greatest modern influence through Marxism, and especially Engels' interpretation. For Engels (1934, 1954), the unity and struggle of opposites was one of the dialectical laws through which change is understood. Without a tension between opposites, things would be unchanging: the overcoming and being overcome of opposing forces explain all natural and human history.

Contemporary Maoism (Mao, Vol. 2, 1965) combines this Western dialectical view of opposites with the classic Chinese perspective. Contradiction—the unity of opposites—is a universal principle explaining change. Things must be studied from the inside, for their development is a self-movement (an imminent causation) due to internal contradictions. One must grasp the principal contradictions, as between proletariat and bourgeoisie in capitalism, to understand the course of change, for it will constitute a struggle between these opposites and the eventual triumph of one over the other.

As a philosophical principle, the unity and struggle of opposites are prominent in my perspective on man and his conflicts. Consider. Perception is the outcome of a struggle between opposing forces—the powers of reality bearing upon us and our outward-directed perspective—between opposing vectors. Reality itself is a complex of opposing powers struggling toward manifestation.

Life is then a struggle of opposites toward realization. Harmony is a balance among such opposites. For society, the struggle is the balancing of powers among men—the manifest determination of their interests, capabilities, and will; the harmony is the structure of expectations. Thus the conflict helix, the process of balancing, balance, disruption, and balancing, is a unity of opposites through which society changes and evolves. Conflict transforms itself into harmony and harmony into conflict; war into peace and peace into war. Both are aspects of the same process, an inseparable unity in the field of man.

9.2 DETERMINISM

In *The Dynamic Psychological Field* (1975) I considered the issue of free will versus determinism. Very briefly, I see man's freedom as a necessary hypothesis of reason. Man can spontaneously decide to act and to initiate new causal series. He can be a first cause.

This freedom, however, lies at the level of potentialities, of things-in-themselves. In the world of manifestations, social interactions, distances, rules, and natural causes, man appears determined, bound inexorably in the process of conflict, in the formation and destruction of structures of expectation. Even though the struggle of opposing interests is ultimately a struggle of an independent will, the elements within the helix—the trigger events, capabilities, credibility, and interests—seem to allow man's will the spontaneity of a leaf floating on the stream of events.

The difficulty here is our simultaneous view of events at two levels. The first is the level of phenomena, of triggers, manifest behavior, specific capability, and determinant distances, where man's behavior appears to be causal and rule following—determined within the conflict helix.

The other level is that of underlying potentialities, dispositions, and powers that we can know only through their transformation into the world of experience. At this level exists man's reason, a potentiality independent of the phenomenological world and with the power to conceive of analytic ideas and moral oughts. At this level we can conceive of man as free.

One and the same social phenomenon can be viewed, therefore, as either free or determined. Located in the phenomenological realm, it is determined by the process of conflict; as a manifestation of man's underlying reason and will, however, it may be reflect man's freedom. These are not inconsistent viewpoints; and both can be valid. Whether one sees an action as free or determined depends on his intentions as a social scientist. If his focus is on the empirical field, the determinate processes, and understanding them, he can deal in forces, causes, conditions, and so on. If, however, his interest is in the moral aspects of the process, in what ought to be and the future man can create through such a process, he can emphasize man's underlying freedom.

All reality may be a struggle of powers. All societies may be arenas of balancing and balanced interests. Strife and harmony may flow into each other like the seasons. But man need not participate. He can withdraw from society, even from reality. If he does not withdraw, *he* can decide when to conflict and what accommodations *he* will accept.

9.3 INEVITABILITY

Is social conflict, then, inevitable? Yes, insofar as man participates in a society, he must establish a balance with others. This is not an empirical statement, as "all history has seen conflict; therefore man must conflict." I am not committing the fallacy of establishing a universal on the basis of empirical knowledge conditioned by time and place (see Popper, 1964). Rather, I am arguing from the essence of man and society. Conflict is intrinsic to man among men. It is a social necessity.

There is no escaping the requirement to come to terms with others, whether lovers or friends, associates or colleagues, antagonists or enemies. And conflict is the process for doing so. Man may be free to decide the how, when, and where of conflict; free to ignore events that would plunge others into strife. Eventually, however, he must assert his interest and realize his power, in order to remain sane.[4]

Is coercive conflict inevitable? Such conflict is manifested when threats, deprivations, and force are used to determine a balance as in strikes, fights, coups, revolutions, and various kinds of warfare. Is such opposition between coercive powers inevitable?

As argued in *The Conflict Helix* (Section 20.2), coercion involves two linked negative interests: if an individual fails to do something he does not want to do (one negative interest), he is threatened with sanctions (the second negative interest). This condition is very much a part of contemporary society. It is an aspect of raising children (do not play with matches, or else . . .), a part of education (if you do not study, you will flunk), an ingredient in modern society's organization (pay your taxes or go to jail), in its everyday regulation (if you drive faster than 35 miles per hour on Haiku Road, you will be fined), and in our jobs (publish or perish). Coercion seems to be pervasive. Is it essential?

I can conceive of raising children without coercion. By manipulating the situation and opportunities of the child, by love, and by the use of authority and bargaining, the parent may avoid threats, spankings, and other negative sanctions. Such is the argument of the permissive school. I can also conceive of friends, lovers, and relatives whose interaction is devoid of coercion.[5]

However I cannot conceive of a large collective of individuals differentiated by interests and roles who can totally avoid coercion. Law-norms enforced by sanctions will always be essential to maintain order within society and to protect individual rights. Even the most authoritative society, such as the Islamic, threatens to cut off the hands of thieves. Those who would eliminate all government coercion and laws, relying exclusively on the exchange between individuals to order society, still make provision for the coercive control of law breakers.

And can love alone organize a society? In the late 1960s many idealistic young people felt that love and altruism and intellectual power (persuasion) were sufficient. They organized communes—small-scale societies in which people could live together cooperatively. To their amazement, coercion became an element in the formation of their structures of expectations. Jobs had to be done, a division of labor had to be developed, and responsibility had to be allocated. Not all participants were equally gifted, equally responsible, or equally interested, and law-norms soon developed to govern the commune. Expulsion from the commune was the final sanction.

Outside the small circle of friends and relatives, we find in the larger society an increasing differentiation of interests and values. Disagreements regarding the proper allocation of rights are inevitable, as is the development of individuals with no moral inhibition against taking what belongs to others. Selfishness, jealousy of others' attainments and property are human traits. The threat of sanctions is the only alternative to a superego inhibiting the expression of such feelings.

Restraining criminals is an obvious and necessary application of coercion. What is not generally recognized is the degree to which modern nontotalitarian society is riven with coercive social conflict unassociated with law-norms. The principal example is the strike. A strike is a coercive instrument, a means of applying deprivation to an employer until he yields to the strikers' demands. Collective bargaining is thus a balancing of coercive powers that establishes a structure of expectations (a contract). Yet like taxes and social security contributions (a coercive government insurance plan), strikes have become accepted as a necessity.

However, as libertarians, classical liberals, and conservatives continue to observe, taxes and strikes (as legalized extortion) are unnecessary; indeed, they inhibit the proper functioning of society. The real argument is not over necessity but over desirability. On the other hand, few but the extreme anarcha-libertarians would deny the need for some kind of coercive protection (private guard corporations or governmental police and court systems) against common crooks and clever thiefs.[6]

Is then the amount of coercion applied in a society a matter of degree? The U.S.S.R. is a more coercive society than Spain, and the latter more than Brazil, which is more coercive than the

United States. Moreover, in terms of government rules and regulations, New York City is a more coercive city than Honolulu, which in turn is more coercive than Houston. But the degrees, as with heating water, become qualitatively transformed. All societies exercise coercion, but there is a meaningful difference between exchange, authoritative, and coercive societies. As discussed in *The Conflict Helix* (Chapter 30), the authoritative and exchange societies apply coercion to protect accepted principles or rights; in the coercive societies the elite apply coercion to organize society toward a superordinate goal. Man cannot escape coercion, thus coercive conflict; but by the society he creates he can determine its scope, amount, and direction.

If conflict is inevitable among men in society, what about violence? Is violence inevitable?

Violence is the use of force, when coercion fails, or the application of deprivations attendant to coercion ("terrorist activities will continue until the regime submits to our demands"). If one accepts the need for coercion, even on a minimal basis to protect people's rights, then force is inevitable. Force is the *ultima ratio.* Unless occasionally used, the threat of sanctions undergirding the law-norms of society is empty. If those who prey on others could do so with impunity, they could protect their illegal gains simply by using force. It would be unreasonable to expect all to refrain from operating outside the law.

But violence takes many forms. Some acts of violence accompany the functioning of law-norms (such as the force applied by the police to restrain a prisoner). Others ensue from collective social conflict, such as riots, terrorism, revolutions, or war.

If one considers all forms of violence, he must conclude that some are inevitable. But when different kinds of collective violence are considered, the answer is less certain. Violence attendant on enforcing even minimal law-norms is a social inevitability based on unavoidable social differentiation and differences in values and interests. Is collective violence also a social inevitability?

At the outset, we must understand that some types of

collective violence are limited to certain societies. For example, war is violence between states in the international society; revolution is a violent, direct attempt to change the elite and their policies within a state-society; civil war is an attempt to violently create a separate state-society. *Thus although we could eliminate one form of violence by altering the social system within which it is defined (as by eliminating war through the institution of world government), we may create another form congenial to the new society (such as civil war or revolution under a world government).* [7] The upshot is that we must deal with collective violence generally, for if the occurrence of one form is not inevitable, some form or another is.

Revolutions, uprisings, riots, wars, coups, assassinations, terrorism have been the lot of all civilizations, cultures, and nations. Toynbee's (1936-1954) massive historical study, Durant's comprehensive survey,[8] or Wells' (1922) popular outline all show that collective violence has always been with man. For the statistical taste, there are Sorokin's (1957) historical tabulations. Man's societies have evolved; knowledge has grown, science has developed, technology has expanded and matured. Only his collective violence has not evolved. The forms we know now were there at the beginning of recorded history, and although I know of no quantitative survey, I have the impression that the extent of violence today is little different from ancient times.[9]

But history is the record of phenomena, of manifestations, of observations. That a phenomenon has always been part of the human record does not prove inevitability. This is not true of certain diseases, now virtually eradicated, that historically plagued man, nor of his presumed physical limits ("man will never fly" or "leave the earth"). Is collective violence different? Is something intrinsic to society reflected in the historical record, mirroring man's free will and nature?

I believe there is. This constant x is man's morality, his practical reason, his superego. Collective violence is organized class violence between collective oughts. Men who share similar interests about how society ought to be structured, about the best policies of government, or how to improve man's lot, organize into groups. Violence between groups is ultimately altruistic or fraternal. It is class violence over what ought to be.[10] It is believed wrong that some are wealthy while many are poor, that private property be taken away, that a minority elite rule, that workers be exploited, that people live in sin, just to give a partial historical list of representing human values. It is true that many, like international mercenaries, participate in collective violence for selfish gain and profit, because of frustrations or to satisfy a need for adventure. But the basis of such collective violence is ultimately a question of which class ought will prevail. *Collective violence is righteous violence.* [11]

This basis, or in terms of the conflict helix, this balancing of powers manifesting violence, is intrinsic to man and his society. It connects his fundamental needs (protectiveness, self-asser- tiveness), morality (superego and self-esteem), and will. For the essence of man's free will is that he can conceive of an ought that does not exist among phenomena.[12]

It is inconceivable that man will not always differ with respect to class memberships held and moralities espoused.[13] Man is willing to risk death and deprivation for what he deems right[14] and will organize to fight for these beliefs.[15] It is therefore a logical conclusion that collective violence in one form or another will always be with us. This is a necessity of man's practical reason and altruism,[16] a necessity of justice, a necessity for the evolution of social man.

The analysis might end here, it would seem, but this is only half the argument. Altruism or righteousness concerns the goals, the motives of man, their interests. Why, however, does violence break out and end, when presumably the altruistic interests remain the same? Moreover, why do societies differ in the amount, period, and degree of collective violence displayed, as between, say, India, the United States, Italy, and Switzerland?

Within societies we can explain the occurrence of violence in terms of the three elements forming the balance of power underlying expectations: interests (especially those comprising the altruistic and fraternal oughts discussed earlier), capability, and will (or, looked at from another's perspective, credibility). Social violence is probable when the structure of expectations moves sharply out of line with underlying interest (oughts, in this case). The status quo is no longer acceptable, no longer can be lived with, and clearly divides supporters and opponents. A *crisis of legitimacy* ensues. This crisis may be at the national, regional, urban, or sectional level. It may be with organization, like the factory, business, government agency, or university. The same process is involved: the structure of agreements, norms, and distribution of rights loses its legitimacy.

But violence will not occur unless the two other elements are unbalanced as well. Capability and will are intrinsically connected. Much capability can be vitiated by lack of will; a strong will can overcome a weakness in capability. Holding will or credibility constant for the moment, violence is encouraged in a *crisis of legitimacy* when the coercive power capability of groups is ambiguous. If supporters of the status quo are clearly superior in capability over opponents whose success is beyond reach, violence will not occur. Violence is a final measurement of relative capability.

Capability, however, is relative to will, to the credibility of the resolve of a person or a group. A participant who lacks credibility, even though he has the stronger capability invites violence. With vast military force and a tremendous arsenal of nuclear weapons, even mighty America, through internal government dissension and lack of resolve and will, can project a helplessness inviting terrorism, and suggesting that a small organized band like the Weathermen can herald a revolution.

In sum, the motive of collective violence is an altruistic or fraternal concern for our fellow man. But the occurrence of violence is due to a crisis of legitimacy, an ambiguity of coercive power between contending groups, and a weakening of credibility. *It is a product of change and is shaped by power* and, of course, a trigger event. But this is the conflict helix. Violence is the final arbiter between oughts, the fundamental instrument for establishing a new structure of expectations, a new legitimacy between passionate moralities, a new status quo, a new class alignment.

But such are the springs to violence within state-societies. While we can say that violence is thus inevitable, its scope and intensity vary among societies. What influences this? Again, I return to my three kinds of society (1976, Chapters 30, 34). The exchange society, through crosscutting and overlapping groups and structures of expectations, segments moralities. Localized violence will occur, but the likelihood of such events turning into collective violence across the society is remote (1976, Sections 32.5, 35.5). Authoritative societies, however, are ordered according to a particular view of what is right and proper, a particular morality. Schism throughout a society is therefore likely as the dominant structure of expectations becomes incongruent with underlying interests (1976, Sections 32.6, 35.6). The coercive society has the greatest potential for violence. One focus of coercive power exists, and its control rests less on legitimacy than on the systematic application of continuous violence against the ruled. This is a balance maintained by coercive capability and credibility within a polarized field of oughts: "You are with us or against us." Let weakness be shown, either in capability or in will, and the society will explode in mass collective violence (1976, Sections 32.7, 35.7).

Collective violence in all societies is inevitable; intense and wide-scale violence is not. Violence itself is a cause for concern because of the extreme difficulty of balancing against injustice the scale on which violence occurs.

NOTES

1. Heraclitus, as quoted in Burnet (1957:136).

2. Bertalanffy (1928).

3. "Philosophy cannot give up its search for a fundamental unity in this ideal world. But it does not confound this unity with simplicity. It does not overlook the tensions and frictions, the strong contrasts and deep conflicts between the various powers of man. These cannot be reduced to a common denominator. They tend in different directions and obey different principles. But this multiplicity and disparateness does not denote discord or disharmony. All these functions complete and complement one another. Each one opens a new horizon and shows us a new aspect of humanity. The dissonant is in harmony with itself; the contraries are not mutually exclusive, but interdependent: 'harmony in contrariety, as in the case of the bow and the lyre' " (Cassirer, 1944:228).

Consider also the work of Nishida Kitaro, perhaps Japan's greatest modern philosopher, who made the unity of opposites a fundamental of his philosophy. See, for example, Nishida (1958).

4. For the argument that nonassertion of power lies at the base of many severe psychological problems, see May (1972).

5. Recall that an ingredient in coercive power is intentionality. We may do certain undesirable things because we dislike making our mate or friend unhappy or

angry. Moreover, a raised eyebrow or a laugh on us may be a potential negative sanction compelling us to act in ways we would otherwise avoid. Such "sanctions" are, however, unintentional. They are the identive power of the other.

6. For an elaboration of such an exchange society, see Rothbard (1973).

7. This is the profound fallacy in the argument that a world government having a monopoly over force would be a way to peace. Under such a government, what used to be war between nations could metamorphasize into some other form of collective violence, such as revolution, guerrilla warfare, or elite terrorism. The domestic history of governments has not been without large-scale collective violence exceeding the violence of war. The question is not one of eliminating international violence through world government, but whether the risks of violence are thereby lessened, and whether other cultural or personal values thus sacrificed are worth the probable increment of peace.

8. Many of the volumes were written with Ariel Durant. For their conclusion about history, see Durant and Durant (1968).

9. We do know that the frequency of war has remained the same since the early 19th century. See Singer and Small (1972) and Richardson (1960b).

10. I am using "class" as developed in *The Conflict Helix* (Chapter 24).

11. See Section 4.4.

12. Many deterministic social scientists who assert that oughts cannot be logically derived from existential statements (is/ought dichotomy) do not realize that this position entails free will. For if phenomena constitute the world of cause and effect, of natural laws, and if man's oughts cannot be derived from phenomena, then some oughts must be a spontaneous product of man's reason. Consider the rights to freedom of religion and of the press, of private property, or to happiness. The value that no man should be the slave of another is not a matter of evolved cultural experience. The enslavement of some by others was once considered the order of nature. Only through the creation of the concept of man's equality by the Jews, its dissemination through Christianity, and collective violence, was the idea of the "rightness" of slavery eventually eroded.

13. Even if a world totalitarian system were to thoroughly brainwash nearly everyone into an antlike society, the elite themselves would have different oughts. And these would lead inexorably to different organizations and eventual violence, such as the total purging of one side by another. The history of modern communist societies shows what can happen. See, for example, Conquest (1968).

14. It is unfortunate that the psychologist and ethologist have had more influence on contemporary scientific views of violence than the humanist. By mistakenly emphasizing aggression and frustration, the noble and dignifying dimension of man's violence has been ignored. Man collectively fights for justice.

15. It is in not recognizing this that classical liberals and current anarcholibertarians commit their major error. If people feel that the authoritative class—those who head private or public organizations—should not be rich, no matter how well earned by merit or by satisfying consumer demands, people will organize to redistribute wealth. Such organized power can be met only by countervailing power, whether of a government or of a private defense organization that in effect functions as a government. The history of the vigilante movements in the American West during the 19th century shows what happens even when state powers are lacking.

16. Again, this is not to deny free will but to acknowledge it. Collective violence is the affirmation of man's freedom. Those who search for the causes of collective violence are therefore picking up the wrong end of the stick. It is through such violence that man asserts his freedom from causal nature.

Chapter 10

INTENTIONAL HUMANISM

Man is his own chief product.

Eisenberg, 1973

Intentional humanism (Rummel, 1975) is the belief that man is free to create his future and is responsible for his past and present. Man intentionally directs his behavior toward a future goal and can freely alter goals and associated behavior. Moreover, it is the belief that man's ideas and knowledge constitute perspectives on reality that are a dynamic balance between his powers and those of reality. Man intentionally alters this perspective consistent with facts and morality, and he chooses a view of man and social reality that emphasizes his creativity, freedom, and responsibility. What, then, is the relationship between intentional humanism and the conflict helix?

The helix is a perspective on society and conflict, a way of looking at man. It is the sociological plane of intentional humanism, as the dynamic psychological field is its psychological plane.

Consider these elements of the helix. First, social relations involve subjective meanings, values, norms, perceptions, and interests. The unique psychological universe of the individual is the point of departure. Objective conditions or forces have social significance and importance only as man gives them meaning in dynamic balance with his powers. Reality, social or otherwise, must inform each individual's perspective. Man is a dynamic, active, creative element in nature and society.

Second, man's powers have many forms. Some, such as identive power, he shares with all other beings, whereas coercive and intellectual powers are peculiar to intentionally guided rational and moral creatures. Power in its social form is intentional, teleological, goal oriented. The dynamic element in man's interaction with others is each man's means for asserting his individuality, his unique being.

Third, as a universe unto himself man has interests (wants, desires, goals) that confront the powers of nature and the interests of other men. The limits and strengths of these external powers and interests can be gauged only through direct confrontation and balancing. Man thrusts himself outward, and only by the external barriers and counterforces he meets, defeats, and is defeated by does he realize his own limits, abilities, and wants. Life is a balance of powers each man achieves alone. No man can blame another for the life he leads.

Fourth, the harmony, peace, cooperation, and solidary interaction man achieves are the result of the dialectical balancing of powers among men. They are the result of a field process, of conflict, of a working out of norms, rules, implicit understandings, agreements, and the like, the consequence of each man's powers being limited by others.

Fifth, no man can decide what the point of balance should be for another. Each knows only his own interests; those of others are traces they leave on the pheonomenal level. We never really know what another believes, thinks, and wants. We relate to another's self only through his assertion of interests, his projection of his powers in opposition to our own. Thus to decide abstractly what another's real interests are in lieu of his asserting them is to make a stab in the dark.

Finally, antifields result from certain goals that require man to behave in concert. Certain tasks require organization. Where the balancing among individuals is severely curtailed by organizations encompassing society, such as the state, and where state coercion is correlated with the ins and outs across social groupings, a class front develops. Society is fractionated across one cleavage, and intense violence is likely. The best way to avoid intense conflict is to enable a diversity of organizations to develop, presenting maximal opportunity for individuals to exchange and alternate authoritative roles.

What ethics are consistent with this view of man as free, creative, responsible, and teleological?

Freedom is the highest value. Only the individual can decide for himself his interests, costs, and ethical constraints. Each person must be maximally free to decide these issues alone and to balance these against nature and others. The structure of expectations resolved through personal interests and calculations is the one most consistent with personal satisfaction and desires.

Social justice is the balance of powers. Justice is an individual question, not a societal one. Indeed, to impose justice through the state in terms of what is best for society, or ultimately good or bad, right or wrong, is to impose the definition of justice by a few on all others. Justice then becomes a matter of who rules, which reduces to who controls the tools of state coercion.

Justice is what each individual thinks is right, and his ability to achieve this in confrontation with other definitions. At the societal level then, social justice is the multiple overlapping balances between these confrontations. In a world of Christians, Moslems, Hindus, and Buddhists; of liberal democrats, communists, fascists, and monarchists; of positivists, existentialists, phenomenologists, and Hegelians; of lawyers, doctors, laborers, and clerks; of Japanese, Burmese, Americans, and Congolese; and of rulers and ruled—who is to judge what is right and just? The individual. Whether in concert with others or through his own powers, the individual's search for justice and the resulting balance against the strivings of others becomes the final definition.

Social justice is maximal freedom. If justice lies in individual interests, morality, and calculations of costs, the more fredom he has to realize his interests and norms, the more social justice. The more an individual can work out his implicit contracts, the more social justice. Social justice, then, lies not in the coercive mechanisms of the state or some other such organization, but in the *lack* of these mechanisms.

Maximal freedom will minimize violence and extreme con-

fict. If people are free to decide their own lives in confrontation with nature and others, maximum diversity is promoted. Diversity of groups, of structures of expectations, of balances, of behavior crosscuts society with multiple alliances, contracts, factions, and conflicts. Society is then truly sewn together by conflict. Moreover, class conflict is segmented, and crosscutting roles, norms, and balances assure that conflict will be drained off before the total society is engaged.

Maximal freedom will check and balance the aggrandizement of coercive power. A weakness in libertarian, anarchist, anti-state, or Marxist literature[1] is the lack of appreciation of Michels' iron law of oligarchy (1949), Acton's principles (1967), and de Jouvenel's historical conclusions about power (1962). All organizations tend to oligarchic power (the right and sanctions of command by an elite); all such power tends to aggrandize itself; all such power will grow unless checked by counterpower; and absolute power corrupts absolutely.

Man is not good. Nor is he evil. Man is fundamentally concerned with his own interests and achieving his own goals. These interests and goals can be egoistic, to be sure. But they can also be fraternal, altruistic, and selfless. Too many have sacrificed personal gain, comfort, and even their lives for the betterment of others to permit one to assert selfishness as a rule. But one man's altruism may be another's prison.

Nonetheless, in a diverse, noncoercively organized society, some will certainly try to assert their desires and ethics over others—that is, to jockey for greater and greater power. A large organization or a government with minimal caretaker functions could increase its power until the diverse elements in society were constrained and partitioned into harmless patches of social fields. The growth of coercive government power in the United States and Great Britain exemplify this. In a society of maximum freedom, what is to prevent some from transforming a power base into a tyranny over all others?

Relevant here are the analyses of Montesquieu, Mosca, de Jouvenel, and others who have seen the absolute requirement for checks and balances. Coercive power checks coercive power. Aggrandizing power limits other aggrandizing powers. It is crucial, then, to equate power with its source. Power is not balanced by dividing it institutionally into a system of checks and balances, as in the United States, and then generating such power from the same source, voting majorities; nor by dividing government into legislative, judicial, and executive brances having separate powers but all appointed by a king. As Mosca so well saw, to check aggrandizing power, power balances must be based on opposing social forces. True opposing interests must be engaged.

The solution to maintaining diversity is inherent in freedom itself. If diversity is enabled to develop and individuals are free to strike their own balances, opposition based on differing interests will curb aggrandizing power. Freedom and diversity are the best check against the growth of a power center. As in the economic world, where a monopoly cannot exist without coercive government support (von Mises, 1963), in a free society a monopoly of power could not develop. Each surge of power would provoke its opposition from different social interests.

The ultimate solution is decentralization. How can intentional humanism be implemented? The solution is not more government, but less; not centralization, but decentralization; not world government, but the breakdown of the sovereign state; not planning, but individual spontaneity and responsibility; not coerced dependence, but balanced interdependence and autonomy. As Nock (1935) points out, our enemy is the state, whether the benevolent welfare state which regulates, legislates, and dictates in the service of some special interests, or the totalitarian state which terrorizes all, controls all, and murders tens of millions in the service of justice as defined by a handful.

The argument of this and the previous volumes ultimately implies the elimination of the state. It implies a total dedication to freedom as the means to justice, truth, and beauty. And it is the means to minimizing violence and war between men.

This may be the appropriate point to end my third volume on man's intentional field. But I would rather conclude on a note of intellectual perplexity. Most social scientists, who generally incline toward socialism or its weaker welfare state version, will be skeptical of my conflict helix perspective and its emphases on the balancing of powers. Emphasizing power is bad enough. Then to link the balance of power and justice? And finally, to cast out the modern democratic state as no longer the bulwark of justice? Surely this is madness.

But then what about the following perspective?

Man has diverse views of reality and conceptions of truth. What he sees is a function of the dialectical conflict between his perspective and the powers of reality to manifest specifics within his perspective. Moreover, part of his perspective comprises his cultural meanings and schema as well as his approach and methods for determining truth. What is truth to an individual is then perspectival; it is the outcome of a conflict between the powers of reality and man's. Moreover, what is social truth—the knowledge of a culture or society—is then dependent on the clash of separate, autonomous truths.

Truth is a balance of diverse perspectives and intellectual powers.

How do we arrive at truth? By providing our grounds, by being public, and by being critical. But criticism implies conflict. Science, for example, is institutionalized conflict for the balancing of powers among diverse views and evidence. The norms of science (freedom to assert one's views, intersubjective testability, public data, precise methods) are the norms for a conflict helix directed at maximizing truth. The process of intellectual and scientific growth is a particularization of the general conflict helix. The powers that are balanced are intellectual and authoritarian; the interests involve facts, theories, beliefs; the structure of expectations then is a settled paradigm.

The outline of intellectual history as a conflict and balancing of ideas should not be too controversial. Most accept today that knowledge grows out of diversity, critical interaction, and conflict. Moreover, once the meaning of intellectual power is understood, *truth is a balance of power.*

Now comes the normative kicker. Because this process is so essential to truth, man must be absolutely free to assert his beliefs, free to try various approaches, free to criticize, debate, disagree. Man must be free in the realm of ideas. At least in the West, there is consensus: the state must not interfere with the freedom of speech and belief; censorship is bad; diversity is good; the free conflict of ideas promotes truth.

A similar argument could be made for beauty. The conflict between aesthetic tastes and demands, the balance between different conceptions of beauty and aesthetic powers, the need and importance of artistic diversity in encouraging creativity, point to a process that is yet another particularization of the conflict helix. And of course, the intellectual chorus would agree, the state must neither define what is beautiful nor interfere in the process.

Surely the process of establishing truth and beauty, the balancing of powers, conceptions, interests, and so on, which underlie them, are sensible and widely accepted. The invocation against state interference and the emphasis on maximal freedom is no less accepted.

My position on justice and the state is precisely the same. The case for truth and beauty holds for justice. Justice is the outcome of a process of balancing of powers. The state must not interfere. Interference means some men imposing their conception of justice on others. A "majoritarian" democratic government makes no difference. If an assumed majority cannot legislate truth or beauty, how can they legislate justice?

From the perspective of the conflict process in the social field, justice is an outcome of a mutual adjustment of interests, capabilities, and credibility. Justice is a balance of powers, a balance of interests. The key to justice is freedom. Its consequence is the best possible peace with justice.

NOTE

1. Marxism is a form of idealistic anarchism: the state is a tool of the bourgeois class. Once this class is eliminated, the need for a state disappears, and men can live cooperative, mutually beneficial lives.

BIBLIOGRAPHY

Acton, Lord. *Essays in the Liberal Interpretation of History,* edited and with an introduction by William H. McNeill. Chicago: University of Chicago Press, 1967.

Alland, Alexander, Jr. *The Human Imperative.* New York: Columbia University Press, 1972.

Ansbacher, Heintz, and Rowena Ansbacher (Eds.). *The Individual Psychology of Alfred Adler.* New York: Harper & Row, 1956.

Ardrey, Robert. *The Social Contract.* New York: Atheneum, 1970.

–––. *The Territorial Imperative.* New York: Atheneum, 1966.

Arendt, Hannah. *The Human Condition.* Chicago: University of Chicago Press, 1958.

–––. *On Violence.* New York: Harcourt Brace Jovanovich, 1969.

Ayer, A. J. *Language, Truth and Logic.* New York: Dover, 1946.

Banfield, Edward C. *The Unheavenly City.* Boston: Little, Brown, 1970.

Bandura, Albert. *Aggression: A Social Learning Analysis.* Englewood Cliffs, N.J.: Prentice-Hall, 1973.

Berelson, Bernard, and Gary A. Steiner. *Human Behavior.* New York: Harcourt Brace Jovanovich, 1964.

Berkowitz, Leonard. *Aggression: A Social Psychological Analysis.* New York: McGraw-Hill, 1962.

Bernard, L.L., *Instinct.* New York: Holt, Rinehart & Winston, 1924.

Bertalanffy, Ludwig. *Nikolaus von Kues.* Munich: G. Muller, 1928.

Birney, Robert C., and Richard C. Teevan (Eds.). *Instinct.* New York: Van Nostrand Reinhold, 1961.

Blau, Peter M. *Exchange and Power in Social Life.* New York: Wiley, 1967.

Bottome, Phyllis. *Alfred Adler; A Biography.* New York: Putnam, 1939.

Burgess, E., and P. Wallin. "Homogamy in Social Characteristics." American Journal of Sociology, Vol. 49 (1943), 109-124.

Burnet, John. *Early Greek Philosophy.* New York: World, 1957.

Burton, J. W. *System, States, Diplomacy and Rules.* New York: Cambridge University Press, 1968.

Buss, A. H. *The Psychology of Aggression.* New York: Wiley, 1961.

Carthy, J. D., and F. J. Ebling (Eds.). *The Natural History of Aggression.* New York: Academic Press, 1964.

Cassirer, Ernst. *An Essay on Man.* New Haven, Conn.: Yale University Press, 1944.

Cattell, Raymond B. *Personality and Motivation.* Yonkers-on-Hudson, N.Y.: World Book, 1957.

–––. *The Scientific Analysis of Personality.* Baltimore, Md.: Penguin Books, 1965.

–––. *A New Morality from Science: Beyondism.* New York: Pergamon Press, 1972.

Cattell, Raymond B., and John L. Horn. *Handbook for the Motivation Analysis Test.* Champaign, Ill.: Institute for Personality and Ability Testing, 1959.

———, and Frank W. Warburton. *Objective Personality and Motivation Tests.* Urbana: University of Illinois Press, 1967.

Coleman, James S. *Introduction to Mathematical Sociology.* New York: Free Press, 1964.

Conquest, Robert. *The Great Terror.* New York: Macmillan, 1968.

Crook, John Hurrell. "The Nature and Function of Territorial Aggression," in Ashley Montagu (Ed.), *Man and Aggression,* 2nd ed. New York: Oxford University Press, 1973, pp. 183-220.

Dahrendorf, Ralf. *Class and Class Conflict in Industrial Society.* Stanford, Calif.: Stanford University Press, 1959.

———. *Essays in the Theory of Society.* Stanford, Calif.: Stanford University Press, 1968.

Davies, James C. "Toward a Theory of Revolution." American Sociological Review, Vol. 27 (1962), 5-19.

———. "The J-Curve of Rising and Declining Satisfaction as a Course of Some Great Revolutions and a Contained Rebellion," in Hugh Davis Graham and Ted Robbert Gurr (Eds.), *The History of Violence in America.* New York: Bantam, 1969.

———. "Violence and Aggression: Innate or Not?" Western Political Quarterly, Vol. 23 (1970), 611-623.

———. "Aggression, Violence, Revolution, and War," in Jeanne N. Knutson, *Handbook of Political Psychology.* San Francisco: Jossey-Bass, 1973, pp. 234-260.

Davis, James A. "Structural Balance, Mechanical Solidarity, and Interpersonal Relations," in Joseph Berger et al. (Eds.), *Sociological Theories in Progress.* Boston: Houghton Mifflin, 1966.

De Kadt, Emanuel J. "Conflict and Power in Society." International Social Science Journal, Vol. 17 (1965), 454-471.

Dollard, J., et al. *Frustration and Aggression.* New Haven, Conn.: Yale University Press, 1939.

Durant, Will. *The Story of Civilization,* Vols. 1-10. New York: Simon & Schuster, 1935-1967.

———. *The Life of Greece.* New York: Simon & Schuster, 1939.

———, and Ariel Durant. *The Lessons of History.* New York: Simon & Schuster, 1968.

Eisenberg, Leon. "The 'Human Nature' of Human Nature," in Ashley Montagu (Ed.), *Man and Aggression,* 2nd ed. New York: Oxford University Press, 1973, pp. 53-69.

Engels, Friedrich. *Herr Engen Dühring's Revolution in Science.* London, 1934.

———. *Dialectics of Nature.* London, 1954.

Eskola, Antti. "Perception of the Basic Cleavages of Finnish Society." Journal of Peace Research, No. 4 (1970), 259-265.

Fletcher, Ronald. *Instinct in Man.* New York: International Universities Press, 1957.

Ford, Donald H., and Hugh B. Urban. *Systems of Psychotherapy: A Comparative Study.* New York: Wiley, 1963.

Fromm, Erich. *The Anatomy of Human Destructiveness.* New York: Holt, Rinehart & Winston, 1973.

Gurr, Ted Robert. "A Comparative Study of Civil Strife," in Hugh Davis Graham and Ted Robert Gurr (Eds.), *Violence in America.* New York: Bantam Books, 1969, pp. 572-632.

―――. *Why Men Rebel.* Princeton, N.J.: Princeton University Press, 1970.

Halebsky, Sandor. "New Perspectives on Political Radicalism." Journal of Political and Military Sociology, Vol. 2 (Spring, 1974), 113-124.

Heider, Fritz. *The Psychology of Interpersonal Relations.* New York: Wiley, 1958.

Himmelweit, T. "Frustration and Aggression: A Review of Recent Experimental Work." In T. H. Pear, (Ed.), *Psychological Factors in Peace and War.* London: Hutchinson, 1950.

Homans, George C. *Social Behavior.* New York: Harcourt Brace Jovanovich, 1961.

Horn, John L. "Motivation and Dynamic Calculus Concepts from Multivariate Experiment," in Raymond B. Cattell (Ed.), *Handbook of Multivariate Psychology.* Skokie, Ill.: Rand McNally, 1966, pp. 625-631.

Horney, Karen. *Our Inner Conflicts.* New York: Norton, 1945.

Hudson, W. D. (Ed.). *The Is/Ought Question.* New York: Macmillan, 1969.

Humphreys, Christmas. *Buddhism,* rev. ed. Baltimore, Md.: Penguin Books, 1955.

Johnson, Chalmers. *Revolutionary Change.* Boston: Little, Brown, 1966.

Johnson, Roger N. *Aggression in Man and Animals.* Philadelphia: W. B. Saunders, 1972.

de Jouvenel, Bertrand D. *On Power,* translated by J. F. Huntington. Boston: Beacon Press, 1962.

Klein, Melanie. *Contributions to Psycho-Analysis.* London: Hogarth, 1950.

Koestler, Arthur. *The Ghost in the Machine.* Chicago: Regnery, 1967.

Lorenz, Konrad. *On Aggression,* translated by Marjorie Latzke. London: Methuen, 1966.

Lupsha, Peter A. "Explanation of Political Violence: Some Psychological Theories Versus Indignation." Politics and Society, Vol. 2 (Fall, 1971), 89-104.

Mao Tse-tung. *Selected Works of Mao Tse-tung,* Vol. 2. Peking: Foreign Language Press, 1965.

May, Rollo. *Power and Innocence.* New York: Norton, 1972.

Megargee, Edwin I. *The Psychology of Violence and Aggression.* Morristown, N.J.: General Learning Press, 1972.

Merton, Robert K. *Social Theory and Social Structure,* rev. ed. New York: Free Press, 1957.

Michels, Robert. *Political Parties.* New York: Free Press, 1949.

Miron, Murray S., and Charles E. Osgood. "Language Behavior: The Multivariate Structure of Qualification," in R. B. Cattell (Ed.), *Handbook of Multivariate Experimental Psychology.* Skokie, Ill.: Rand McNally, 1966.

von Mises, Ludwig. *Human Action,* 3rd ed. Chicago: Regnery, 1963.

Montagu, Ashley (Ed.). *Man and Aggression,* 2nd ed. New York: Oxford University Press, 1973.

Mowrer, O. H. *Learning Theory and Personality Dynamics.* New York: Ronald Press, 1950.

Nieburg, H. L. "The Threat of Violence and Social Change." American Political Science Review, Vol. 56 (December 1962), 865-873.

Nishida, Kitaro. *Intelligibility and the Philosophy of Nothingness: Three Philosophical Essays,* translated by R. Schinzinger. Tokyo, 1958.

Nock, Albert Jay. *Our Enemy, The State.* New York: Morrow, 1935.

Osgood, Charles E., George J. Suci, and Percey H. Tannenbaum. *The Measurement of Meaning.* Urbana: University of Illinois Press, 1957.

Parkman, Margaret, and Jack Sawyer. "Dimensions of Ethnic Intermarriage in Hawaii." American Sociological Review, Vol. 32 (August 1967), 593-607.

Popper, Karl R. *The Poverty of Historicism.* New York: Harper & Row, 1964.

Portes, Alejandro. "On the Logic of Post-Factum Explanations: The Hypothesis of Lower-Class Frustration as the Cause of Leftist Radicalism," in Philip Brickman (Ed.), *Social Conflict. Lexington, Mass.: D. C. Heath, 1974, pp. 398-420.*

———, and Adreain Ross. "A Model for the Prediction of Leftist Radicalism." Journal of Political and Military Sociology, Vol. 2 (Spring 1974), 33-56.

Rapoport, Anatol. *Fights, Games, and Debates.* Ann Arbor: University of Michigan Press, 1960.

Rashevsky, N. *Mathematical Theory of Human Relations.* Bloomington, Ind.: Principia Press, 1949.

Richardson, Lewis F. *Arms and Insecurity.* Pittsburgh: Boxwood Press, 1960.

———. *Statistics of Deadly Quarrels.* Pittsburgh: Boxwood Press, 1960b.

Rothbard, Murray. *For a New Liberty.* New York: Macmillan, 1973.

Rotter, J. B. *Social Learning and Clinical Psychology.* Englewood Cliffs, N.J.: Prentice-Hall, 1954.

Rummel, R. J. *Applied Factor Analysis.* Evanston, Ill.: Northwestern University Press, 1970.

———. *Dimensions of Nations.* Beverly Hills, Calif.: Sage, 1972.

———. *The Dynamic Psychological Field.* New York: Halsted (a Sage Publications book), 1975.

———. *The Conflict Helix.* New York: Halsted (a Sage Publications book), 1976.

Runciman, W. G. *Relative Deprivation and Social Justice.* Berkeley: University of California Press, 1966.

Scott, J. P. "The Old-Time Aggression," in Ashley Montagu (Ed.), *Man and Aggression,* 2nd ed. New York: Oxford University Press, 1973, pp. 136-143.

Simon, Herbert. *Models of Man.* New York: Wiley, 1957.

Singer, J. David, and Melvin Small. *The Wages of War, 1816-1965.* New York: Wiley, 1972.

Sokal, Robert R., and Peter H. A. Sneath. *Principles of Numerical Taxonomy.* San Francisco: W. H. Freeman, 1963.

Sorokin, Pitirim. *Social and Cultural Dynamics,* Vols. 1-IV. Boston: Porter Sargent, 1937-1941.

———. *Social and Cultural Dynamics,* rev. abr. ed. Boston: Porter Sargent, 1957.

———. *Society, Culture and Personality.* New York: Cooper Square, 1969.

Sperlich, Peter W. *Conflict and Harmony in Human Affairs.* Skokie, Ill.: Rand McNally, 1971.

Storr, Anthony. *Human Aggression.* New York: Atheneum, 1968.

Tinbergen, N. *The Study of Instinct.* Oxford: Clarendon Press, 1951.
Toynbee, A. J. *A Study of History,* Vols. 1-10. Oxford: Oxford University Press, 1936-1954.

Watanabe, Satoshi (Ed.). *Methodologies of Pattern Recognition.* New York: Academic Press, 1969.
Wells, H. G. *The Outline of History,* 3rd ed. New York: Macmillan, 1922.
White, Ralph K. "Misperception and the Vietnam War." Journal of Social Issues, Vol. 22 (July 1966).

Yates, Aubrey J. *Frustration and Conflict.* New York: Wiley, 1962.

Zeitlin, Irving M. *Rethinking Sociology.* Englewood Cliffs, N.J.: Prentice-Hall, 1973.
Zimmer, Heinrich. *Philosophies of India.* Princeton, N.J.: Princeton University Press, 1969.

NAME INDEX

Acton, Lord, 182
Adler, Alfred, 36, 64-6
Alland, Alexander, Jr., 41
Ansbacher, Heintz, 37, 64
Ansbacher, Rowena, 37, 64
Aquinas, St. Thomas, 112
Ardrey, Robert, 64
Arendt, Hannah, 64
Aristotle, 112
Ayer, A. J., 129

Banfield, Edward C., 92
Bandura, Albert, 40, 65, 70, 91
Berelson, Bernard, 136
Berkowitz, Leonard, 85
Bernard, L. L., 64
Bertalanffy, Ludwig, 177
Birney, Robert C., 64
Blau, Peter M., 127
Bottome, Phyllis, 65
Burgess, E., 136
Burnet, John, 167, 177
Burton, J. W., 87
Buss, A. H., 85

Carthy, J. D., 64
Cassirer, Ernst, 177
Cattell, Raymond B., 52, 55, 66, 91
Coleman, James S., 163
Conquest, Robert, 178
Crook, John Hurrell, 64

Dahrendorf, Ralf, 97, 100-2, 109
Davies, James C., 74-6
Davis, James A., 112, 136
DeKadt, Emanuel J., 97
Dollard, J., 65, 69
Durant, Ariel, 178
Durant, Will, 167, 174, 178
Durkheim, E., 113, 136, 143

Ebling, F. J., 64
Eisenberg, Leon, 179
Engels, Friedrich, 168

Fletcher, Ronald, 64
Ford, Donald H., 65
Freud, Sigmund, 37, 56, 64-5
Fromm, Erich, 38, 55-6, 64-6, 85

Gluckman, Max, 139
Gurr, Ted, 71-7, 84-6, 163

Halebsky, Sandor, 86
Heider, Fritz, 112, 136
Heraclitus, 111, 167, 177
Himmelweit, T., 85
Homans, George, 127
Horn, John L., 66
Horney, Karen, 65
Hudson, W. D., 137
Hume, David, 122, 129
Humphreys, Christmas, 168

Johnson, Chalmers, 145, 150-4
Johnson, Roger N., 64
de Jouvenal, Bertrand D., 182

Kant, Immanuel, 130
Klein, Melanie, 38
Koestler, Arthur, 91-2

Lorenz, Konrad, 34, 40, 56, 65-6
Lupsha, Peter A., 92

MacIver, R. M., 113
Mao, Tse-tung, 167-8
Marx, Karl, 145, 149-50
May, Rollo, 36, 64, 66, 144, 177
Megargee, Edwin L., 65, 85
Merton, Robert K., 127, 137

SUBJECT INDEX

aggression, 25, 116, 178; altruistic, 47; assertive, 45; authoritative, 47; and bargaining, 46; and behavior, 49; benign, 38, 55; definition of, 50; hostility, 49; identive, 44, 51-3; intellectual, 47; malignant, 39, 66; manipulative, 48; the psychological field of, 61-2; and power, 44-8; and violence, 48-9. See also frustration.

altruism, 175. See also aggression.

anger, 54-5

anomie, 27, 143-4

antagonism, 112-7, 126, 135-6

antifield, 15, 22, 140, 142, 180

arms race, 154, 156

attitudes, 56-9, 103, 131-2, 135

authority, 101-2, 104, 107-9, 143, 152, 154; authoritarian, 20. See also aggression, power, society.

awareness, 160

beauty, 185

behavior, 13, 15, 41, 60; equation of, 13. See also aggression, conflict, disposition.

class, 17, 75-6, 84, 93, 133-4, 140-1, 143, 149-9, 160, 175, 178, 180; consciousness, 104-5; definition of, 98; interests of, 98, 105; struggle, 92. See also conflict, violence.

coercion, 46, 171-3, 182. See also society.

conflict, behavior, 19; class, 182; dimensions of, 22; helix, 19, 23, 27, 36, 62-4, 83-5, 102-6, 134-6, 144, 148, 150, 152-3, 156-7, 160, 162, 169, 179; latent, 148, 150; model of, 150; of opposites, 27; political, 107; pro-

positions of, 21-2; realistic, 88; situation of, 17, 135; space of, 17, 124; structure of, 17, 135. See also antagonism, crime, hostility, revolution, strike, threat, violence, war.

credibility, 19, 156, 160, 175

crime, 163

cross-pressures, 26, 139-41

crowding, 64

culture, 42-3, 57-60, 65, 116; ideational, 147, 161; lag of, 159; sensate, 147, 161; space of, 131-3

cycles, 161-3

density, 144

deprivation, 26, 70-6

determinism, 28, 169-70

dimensions. See conflict.

dispositions, 13; behavioral, 58-61, 66

dissonance, 26, 89

distance, 132, 134; political, 134; social, 15; sociocultural, 80; vector of, 123, 125, 131, 135

dominance, 51; temperament, 52, 66

drives, 53-4

economic development, 21

education, 21

ego, 56

environment, 57

equality, 75-6, 79, 119

equilibrium theory, 98

eros, 37-8

essence, 119, 121, 123, 137

ethics, 129-30, 132-4

ethology, 35, 64

exchange. See society.

expectations, 13, 26, 58-61, 66, 74, 77, 83, 90-1, 127-8, 135, 142, 149, 156;